Burglars in The Yard

Sheila K. McCullagh

Illustrated by Ray Mutimer

Nelson

Tim and his friends, Arun, Jessica and Simon, all live in houses in The Yard, in a big town.

All four of them have magic tokens (silver coins or a silver key). When they are wearing their magic tokens, they can see the Hidden People — the people nobody else can see. There is Melinda, the 'safe' witch who can work magic; Tobias, the cat who can fly a broomstick, and Sebastian, Tim's cat, who is one of the Strange Ones; Captain Jory and the Hidden People who live in Hollow Hill; Jared, the boy they saved from the wild witches; and many others.

This is another of Tim's adventures among the Hidden People.

Chapter One

"Tim! Hi, Tim!" Simon ran across The Yard, as Tim came through the gap in the houses that led to Canal Road.

"Hallo, Simon," said Tim. "What's up?"

"Jess can't come tonight," said Simon. "She's got flu. She'll have to stay in bed. But I'm all right. I'm coming."

"Don't you think we'd better call it off, till Jessica's better?" Tim said. "Arun's away, too."

"Jess doesn't mind if I go," said Simon. "She says she'll be all right. And I've been looking forward to it all week."

Tim had promised to take Simon and Jessica out that night. Captain Jory, one of the Hidden People, was running a load of goods down the canal to Hollow Hill. He had told Tim that the three of them could go with him. An old, black barge was already tied up to the canal bank, just below the bridge, ready to start as soon as the moon came up.

"Won't they miss you?" asked Tim.

Simon shook his head.

"We don't start till nearly midnight, do we?" he asked. "Uncle Joe and Auntie Lizzie are going out. They always go out on Saturday nights. But it wouldn't matter, even if they were in. They never come up to see us, once we're in bed."

"All right, if you're sure," said Tim. "We'll be away three or four hours. Tobias will bring us back from Hollow Hill."

Simon gave a little jump of excitement. Tobias the cat was one of the Hidden People, and he could fly a broomstick. If Tobias was going with them it meant that they would fly.

"Where shall I meet you?" asked Simon.

"I'll come and pick you up from your bedroom window, with Tobias," said Tim. "We'll take a broomstick, and if Tobias is with us, he'll make sure that we're invisible."

"Do you mean that no one will be able to see us?" asked Simon.

"The Hidden People will be able to see you, all right — but not Ordinary Folk," said Tim.

"Didn't you know? Tobias' magic is so strong, that he can always make you invisible to Ordinary Folk, when he wants to."

"Can Sebastian?" asked Simon. Sebastian was Tim's cat.

"No," said Tim. "Sebastian can fly a broomstick, but his magic isn't nearly as strong as Tobias'. That's why Tobias is coming tonight. No one must see us on that barge. You be ready just before midnight. You'll see."

Simon gave another little jump of excitement. Then he ran off, back to the house where he lived with his uncle and aunt, and Jessica, his sister.

Tim went over to the house opposite Simon's, where he lived with his Aunt May. Aunt May had her bedroom in the basement, and Tim had his in the attics, with lodgers living in between.

He shut the front door behind him, and went down to the kitchen, blowing on his hands.

Aunt May took one look at him, and put a saucepan on the stove.

"Come and sit by the fire and get warm," she said. "You look frozen. And no gloves! Why don't you put your gloves on? I've got some hot soup for tea tonight, and we'll have it right away. I don't want you getting flu. There's a lot of it about."

"Simon said that Jessica's got flu," said Tim, sitting down and holding out his hands to the fire.

"I'm not surprised," said Aunt May. "That

aunt of hers doesn't look after her properly. She's never in. I'm sure that child doesn't get enough to eat."

"They have a hot meal in the evening, same as we do," said Tim.

"Sausage rolls!" said Aunt May scornfully. "I've seen them buying them. Good hot soup is what you need, in weather like this. I shouldn't be surprised if it snowed tonight. It's cold enough.

"Here — you drink this. This will warm you up."

She poured the soup from the saucepan into two big mugs, and handed one to Tim. "Have a bit of toast to dip in it. I've only just made it."

Tim warmed his hands on the mug, and then took a piece of toast and began to eat it, dipping it in the hot soup. The toast broke off, and he got a spoon to spoon it out.

"I'm going out myself tonight," said Aunt May. "I promised Miss Flint that I'd take her along to the Bingo." (Miss Flint was one of the lodgers. She was an old lady, and she didn't get out very much, so Aunt May was trying to cheer her up.) "I expect you'll be in bed by the time I get back. They don't often finish before ten."

"All right," said Tim. "I've got some homework to do, anyway."

"Well, you get to bed in good time," said Aunt May. "You're looking a bit tired."

It was quite dark by the time they had finished the high tea, which was their evening meal. Aunt May went into the room at the back, to get ready to go out. Tim washed up, and then got out his homework. Aunt May went out.

*   *   *

Tim went up to bed about eight o'clock. It was cold, up in the attic.

He opened a drawer, and took out a silver coin, with a hole in the middle. The coin hung on a thin silver chain. Tim hung the chain round his neck, and pushed the coin under his sweater. He needed to wear his magic token, so that he would be able to see the Hidden People.

He didn't undress. He kicked off his shoes and climbed into bed as he was. He pulled the bedclothes up over him. He wanted to get some sleep before he went out, if he could. He knew that Tobias would wake him, when it was time to go.

But somehow or other, Tim couldn't get to sleep. He kept wondering where Sebastian was. Sebastian often slept on Tim's bed, but he wasn't there now.

"I expect he's out, doing something for Melinda," Tim said to himself.

He kept thinking about Captain Jory and the smugglers, too. They had loaded the barge on Friday night. He had seen the cases stacked on it only that morning. They would leave just before midnight, unless there was anyone about. Nobody would be able to see the Hidden

People, but they could see the barge. If they saw the barge going down the canal, with no one on it, people might think it was adrift.

Tim wondered whether he was right to take Simon. Simon was two years younger than he was, and Tim felt responsible for him.

"Still, we can always fly home with Tobias if anything happens," he said to himself.

At last, Tim dropped into an uneasy sleep. He was dreaming about a dragon, when he woke with a start to find something standing on the foot of his bed.

It was very dark. The street lamp in The Yard had gone out, but he could just make out the black shape of a cat in the darkness.

"Tobias?" he asked.

He struck a match, and lit the candle on the table by his bed.

The candle-light shone on Tobias' black fur and bright green eyes. The window was wide open. Tim shivered as he felt the cold air.

"Hallo, Tim," said Tobias. "Are you ready? Captain Jory's just leaving."

"Just a moment," said Tim.

He scrambled out of bed, put on his shoes, and picked up his anorak. He pushed his arms into it, grabbed his gloves, and went over to the window.

"We've got to pick up Simon," he said. "Jessica's not coming. I said we'd pick him up from his bedroom window. That's the one at the back. It looks out over the canal."

"All right," said Tobias. "But be quick."

He jumped on to the window sill, and then outside. A broomstick was floating in the air, level with the sill. Tobias landed on one end.

Tim blew out the candle. He climbed through the window after Tobias and settled himself on the broomstick.

"All set, Tobias," he said.

Tobias waved his tail, and the broomstick moved out, over The Yard. Tim looked down. The moon was hidden behind clouds, and there was very little light.

For a moment, Tim thought that he saw someone outside a house in one corner of The Yard. But then he saw that it was just the white 'For Sale' notice. The notice had been up for weeks. Tim peered down into the darkness. There was no one below.

The broomstick swept up over the roofs of the houses opposite, and came to rest outside Simon's bedroom window. The window was open, and Simon was there, looking out.

"I'm all ready," he whispered excitedly, beginning to climb on to the sill. "I'm wearing my silver coin."

"Have you got your warm things on? It's as cold as Christmas out here," said Tim, shivering a little.

"I've got my anorak on, and my scarf," said Simon.

"You'd better have gloves," said Tim. "Your hands will get frozen, hanging on to the broomstick."

"I've got my gloves in my pocket. I'll put

them on as we go," said Simon.

He slid on to the broomstick just in front of Tim. Tobias waved his tail, and the broomstick moved off. Simon pulled out his gloves. He put one on, but he fumbled with the other. It slipped out of his hand, and dropped into the darkness.

"Blow!" he said. "I've lost it."

"Let's go down for it," said Tim. "You'll need it tonight."

"There isn't much time," said Tobias over his shoulder. "Captain Jory won't be very pleased, if we're late."

"I'd never find it in the dark, anyway," said Simon. "I can put one hand in my pocket."

"The glove fell into Mr. Berryman's garden," said Tim. "We can get it on the way back. But you'll be cold."

"I'll be all right," said Simon.

The broomstick swept down to the canal. The barge was already swinging out across the water. Captain Jory stood at the tiller, and Jack, one of the smugglers, was on the bank, waiting to cast off.

Tobias took the broomstick out over the water, and they dropped off it, into the barge. Tobias put the broomstick down on the deck.

"You're a bit late," said Captain Jory. "Where's Jessica?"

"She's got flu," said Simon. "She wanted to come, but she isn't well enough."

"She can come another time," said Captain Jory. He looked along the canal bank. "What's that over there, Jack? Right down there, along the road? Can you see?"

"Someone's coming," said Jack in a whisper.

"Put the street lights out, Tobias," said Captain Jory softly. "Hold the barge for a minute, Jack. Don't cast off yet. Let her swing round."

The street lamps all down Canal Road suddenly went out. The barge swung slowly in towards the bank again.

They stood still, listening and peering into the darkness.

"Someone's coming, all right," Jack whispered.

They could hear voices now. Two figures were coming along the side of the canal in the darkness just ahead of them.

"Hallo, what's this?" they heard someone say.

"It looks like a barge," said the other.

One of them switched on a torch. He shone the light on to the barge.

"Put that out, you fool!" said the other. "Do you want everyone to see us?"

Tim took a quick breath. He knew who the two were. Their names were Jim and Kevin, and Tim had had trouble with them before. Kevin was Tim's age, and Jim was his older brother. They had once tried to throw Tim into the canal, but two of the Hidden People had helped him. It was Jim and Kevin who had ended up in the canal that time.

Tim hadn't seen them for a long time. He had heard that they had left the town. It looked as if they had come back.

"I'm going on board," said Jim. "It looks to me as if the barge is loaded, ready for the morning. We might find something interesting."

He was just going to jump down, when Kevin said: "Look out! There's a police car."

A police car swung on to the far side of the bridge across the canal. It came over the bridge and turned right, away from them.

"Better leave it," said Kevin. "They'll be back before long. They always patrol this road. They're bound to stop and look at a loaded barge."

Jim hesitated. "I hate to miss a chance like this," he said.

"You don't want to get caught again," said Kevin. "Not after last time."

The moon came out from behind a cloud, and shone down on the barge.

Jack was standing quite still on the bank, only two or three metres away from the two boys. Simon held his breath.

Jim stared down at the barge. Simon was standing just opposite him. He seemed to be looking straight through him. Simon could scarcely believe that Jim couldn't see him.

But Tobias' magic was working well. Jim turned away.

Simon softly let his breath go.

"You win," said Jim. "We'll go on. We want somewhere off the main road. I'd like to find somewhere before the lights come on again.

13

It's a bit of luck, that they've gone off. If only the moon goes in again, we'll be all right."

Jim and Kevin went on down the road.

"They're going into The Yard," Simon whispered softly.

"I wonder what on earth they're after," Tim muttered.

Captain Jory waited until Jim and Kevin had gone through the gap in the houses. Then he turned to Jack.

"Cast off," he said. "We'll be gone by the time they're back. They'll think someone was on board, after all — or perhaps just came along and moved her."

Jack cast off, and jumped on board.

They moved out into the middle of the canal.

"Where's the engine?" whispered Simon.

"There isn't one," said Tim softly. "They work some kind of magic. I don't know how they do it, but it works all right. I've been before."

Clouds blew over the moon again, and as they moved down the canal, Tim and Simon could see the shapes of the houses and factories on each side.

It was very cold. Simon kept his bare hand in his pocket, but he was too excited to bother about it much.

After a time, there were big factories on each side of them. Sometimes they saw lighted windows. They came to a pipe pouring water into the canal. They went past the fairground. There was no one about at all.

At last they left the town behind them, and Simon could see that there was grass along the bank. He could see trees, black against the sky. The barge began to move more quickly.

"Not far to Hollow Hill now," said Captain Jory, as they passed a farmhouse. "I wonder why they're up?"

One window of the house shone brightly in the darkness. But as they watched it, the light went out.

"Lock gates ahead!" said Jack.

"How do they work the gates?" Simon whispered to Tim.

"By magic," said Tim. "You'll see. There's no one there, this time. Last time, two people were sitting on the gates. Jack had to scare them off."

"I'll bet they never came back," said Simon.

Captain Jory laughed.

"Well, we haven't seen anyone here again," he said. "Not at this time of night."

They came to the lock gates. The gates opened for the barge. They moved into the lock, and the gates closed behind them.

Water rushed in, filling the lock. Then the gates on the far side opened. They moved on again, along the canal.

Tim saw an animal trotting along the path on the bank. At first he thought it was a dog, but then the moon came out, and he saw that it was a fox. He touched Simon's arm, and pointed.

Simon caught his breath.

"I've never seen a fox before," he whispered.

The fox heard him. He looked quickly across at the barge, and turned off the path, into the bushes.

A big white owl flew up from one of the trees, and swept down over the barge. It glided away into the darkness.

"I wonder if that's one of Melinda's messengers," said Simon. "I'm sure my owl takes messages for her."

Melinda, the safe witch, had given Simon an owl. It was a little owl made from a magic ivory, and it came alive in the moonlight. Simon had let it fly several times. It always came back. Simon often wondered where it went.

"There's Hollow Hill," said Tim. "They've lit a fire on the hill. Look!"

They could see the flames of a wood fire leaping up in the circle of trees that crowned

Hollow Hill.

"I hope that's not the witches," said Tim.

"No, they've gone," said Jack cheerfully. "No need to worry about them. The Hidden People light a fire on Hollow Hill, if we're running a cargo."

The moon went behind a cloud again. Something that looked like a little white feather drifted down in front of them. Then another came, and another.

"Snow!" said Tim. "Aunt May said it was cold enough."

"She was right," said Simon, dancing about to warm his feet.

Soon, the air was full of falling flakes. The banks on either side of them began to turn white.

"You'd better go back now," said Captain Jory. "You'll be frozen where you stand, if you stay much longer."

"We must just see the Hidden People come out of Hollow Hill," said Tim.

"Well, there they are, then," said Captain Jory. "Look!"

They were almost opposite Hollow Hill now. They could just make it out, through the falling snow. There was a light in the side of the hill, where the door was open. People were coming out of the door, and across the grass towards them.

There were women with cloaks wrapped around them. There were men in three-cornered hats, like the one Captain Jory wore.

There were seamen, too, in stocking caps, like Jack, with earrings in their ears. They came running across towards the barge.

"All friends of yours," said Captain Jory. "But you'd better go now. There's nothing more. We've just got to carry all the stuff up to the hill. Come and see us another time, when it's not so cold. Are you ready with that broomstick, Tobias?"

Tobias jumped on to one end of the broomstick, and floated it just above the deck.

"Come on, Simon," said Tim. "We'd better get back."

"Can we fly over the hill?" asked Simon.

"I expect so," said Tim. "Can we, Tobias?"

"I'll take you if you come now," said Tobias. "But you'd better be quick, if you don't want to walk home. I don't like being out in the snow."

Tim and Simon sat on the broomstick.

"Thanks for the trip, Captain Jory," said Tim.

"It was fantastic," said Simon.

Captain Jory waved his hand. "Come again in the summer," he said.

Tobias waved his tail, and the broomstick flew up across the canal, over the heads of the Hidden People. They looked up and waved, as Tobias flew the broomstick swiftly towards Hollow Hill.

Tim thought that Tobias must be in a good mood, in spite of the snow, or he would have taken them straight home.

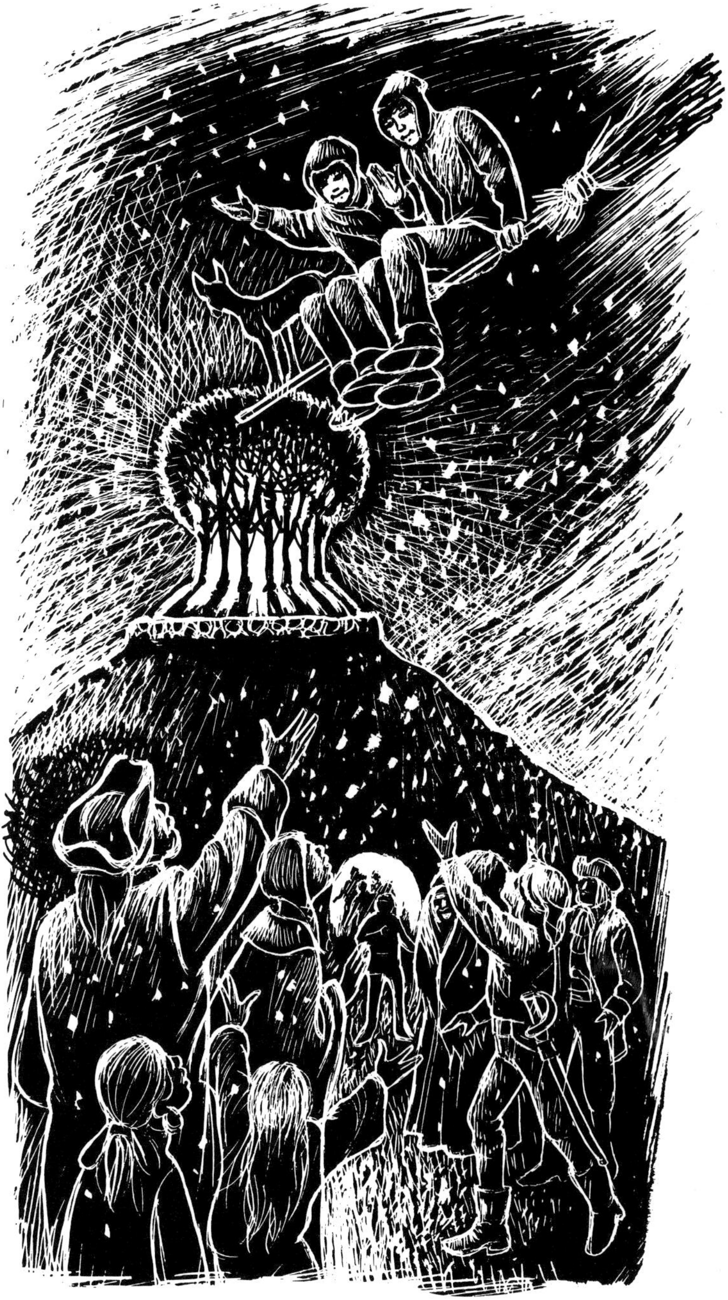

They swept up into the air, and over Hollow Hill. Tim and Simon looked down, and saw the fire below them. It was in the ring of trees, right on the top of the hill. A boy was beside it, and he looked up and waved as they flew by.

"There's Jared!" cried Simon.

Jared was one of the Hidden People. Jessica had rescued him from the wild witches.

Tim and Simon waved back. Tobias turned the broomstick. They circled the hill, and headed back towards the town.

"It's getting thicker," said Tim.

The snow was driving into their faces, and they could see very little below them.

"We'll have a great time tomorrow, making snowballs," said Simon. "And we could go tobogganing — if we had a toboggan. Jess and I used to have one, but I don't know where it is now."

Tobias flew lower. They could make out the black water of the canal below them, with white banks on either side. Soon, they were over the town.

Simon did his best to keep his hand in his pocket, but it still felt very cold. Even the hand with a glove on it was cold.

They saw the police car below them, moving slowly along Canal Road. The snowflakes were lit by the car's headlights. The whole air seemed full of snow.

Tobias swung the broomstick across the road, and brought it up to Simon's window sill.

"Careful," said Tim. The window sill was thick with snow.

"Brrr! It's cold," said Simon, as he clambered in. "Thanks, Tobias. See you in the morning, Tim."

"Goodnight," said Tobias.

He lifted the broomstick up and over the roof of the house. They flew across The Yard, to Tim's window.

"Come in for the night, Tobias," said Tim. "You won't want to go back in this."

"I want to get back to Hollow Hill," said Tobias. "They'll have a feast tonight, with all the stuff that Captain Jory brought."

Tim climbed in at his window.

"Thank you for the ride, anyway, Tobias," he said. "It was great. I'm sorry you've had the snow. Goodnight. Have a good feast."

"I will," said Tobias. "Goodnight, Tim."

He twitched his tail, and the broomstick disappeared into the falling snow.

Tim shut the window. It wasn't snowing as hard as it had been.

The street light in The Yard below came on. Tim looked down. The snow was lying thickly on the ground, and on the branches of the old tree. But as he watched, the clouds parted, and the moon came out.

Tim shivered.

"Time for bed," he said to himself.

He undressed quickly and got into his pyjamas. There was no sign of Sebastian, but that didn't surprise him. If Sebastian was with Melinda when the snow began, he wouldn't be home till morning.

Tim climbed into bed, pulled the bedclothes up around his ears, and went to sleep.

Chapter Two

When Jessica woke up, it was still dark, but the room seemed brighter than usual.

"I wonder if Simon's back," she thought.

She got out of bed, and went over to the window. The world outside was covered in snow. The old tree in the middle of The Yard looked as if all its branches had been spread with white icing, and the roofs of the houses each had a soft white blanket of snow over them. She looked down into the whiteness of The Yard below. There was no one about. Everything was still.

Jessica shivered. It was cold in her attic bedroom. She put on her slippers and dressing gown, and went across the landing to Simon's room. She opened the door softly, and looked in.

She could see a hump in Simon's bed. She tiptoed over to it. Simon was under the bedclothes, fast asleep. Only the top of his head and his nose were showing. Jessica tiptoed out again. She shut the door softly behind her, and went back to bed. She didn't feel very well, but she felt better than she had felt the night before. Now that she knew Simon was safely back, she thought she could go back to sleep.

When Jessica woke again, it was daylight outside. She heard footsteps on the stairs leading up to the attic.

The door opened, and Auntie Lizzie came in. Auntie Lizzie was in her dressing gown. She had a bowl in her hand.

"How are you, Jessica?" she asked, as she came in.

"All right," said Jessica.

"Don't be silly," said Auntie Lizzie. "You're not all right yet. Do you feel any better?"

"Yes," said Jessica. "My headache's gone."

"That's a step in the right direction," said Auntie Lizzie. "You stay in bed today, and we'll see how you are tomorrow. I've brought you some hot bread and milk."

"Thank you," said Jessica.

"Well, you eat it," said Auntie Lizzie. "Uncle Joe's going to bring an electric fire up. You've got to keep warm."

She set the bowl down on the table by Jessica's bed and went out.

Jessica had just finished the bowl of milk,

when Uncle Joe came in with the electric fire.

"Well, Jessica, how are you?" he asked.

"Much better," said Jessica. She was beginning to like Uncle Joe.

"You take care of yourself," he said. He pushed the plug into the socket on the wall, and turned on the fire.

"There — that'll be warmer for you," he said. "But don't go getting out of bed. Keep warm till you're better. It's lucky that I'm working nights. I'll be home all day. If I wasn't working nights, Simon would have had to stay at home to look after you, and I don't want him to miss school."

"I'll be all right," said Jessica.

"Well, we'll keep you at home till you are," said Uncle Joe.

He went downstairs again.

It was an hour later before the door opened again. This time, it was Simon who looked in.

"Hallo, Jess. How are you?" he asked.

"Better," said Jessica. "How did you get on?"

"It was fantastic," Simon said. "Tobias flew us home on a broomstick, in all that snow. And we saw Jared. The Hidden People had lit a fire on the top of Hollow Hill, and he was up there."

"I do wish I could have gone," said Jessica.

"Captain Jory said he'd take you another time," said Simon. "It was pretty cold.

"Auntie Lizzie told me to keep away from you, because of the flu. But I'll look in and see you again. I'm going over to see Tim now. I'll be back soon."

He ran downstairs, leaving the door ajar. Jessica got out of bed to shut it. She went over to the window and looked out.

She saw Simon come out of the house below her, and run across The Yard in the snow to Tim's house. Tim opened the door, and Simon went in.

Jessica was just going back to bed, when a police car came into The Yard. It stopped outside Mr. Berryman's house, and two policemen got out. They went up the steps and knocked on the door. Mr. Berryman opened it, and they went in.

"I wonder what that's about," Jessica said to herself. She liked Mr. Berryman. She had only met him once or twice in The Yard, but he was always very cheerful.

She waited by the window for a while, but the policemen didn't appear again, so she went back to bed.

* * *

Over in Tim's house, Simon looked out of the attic window just in time to see the policemen go into Mr. Berryman's.

"Hi! Come and look, Tim," he said. "There's a police car."

Tim came over to the window.

"I hope Mr. Berryman's all right," he said.

"Let's go outside," said Simon. "It's a waste

to stay indoors, anyway, when there's snow. And we might find out what's happening."

"Tim!" Aunt May called up the stairs. "Tim! Could you shovel out a bit of a pathway? And get the snow off the steps? Miss Flint won't be able to go out, unless you clear it a bit. And she goes to dinner with her cousin on Sundays."

"All right," Tim called back. "We're just coming."

He put on his anorak and gloves.

"Come on, Simon," he said. "You can help, too."

They went downstairs. Tim got two shovels and a broom from the shed in the back yard, and they set to work. Tim shovelled a pathway along the pavement, while Simon brushed the snow off the steps.

Simon stopped to make a snowball and throw it at Tim. Tim threw one back, and for a minute or two the air was thick with snowballs. Tim was a better shot than Simon, and Simon ran off, laughing.

"Come on back and do those steps," Tim said, picking up the shovel again.

He saw Simon's hands.

"Haven't you got another pair of gloves?" he asked.

One of Simon's hands was still bare.

"No," said Simon. "But it doesn't matter. I'll be warm enough, doing this."

The two policemen came out of Mr. Berryman's house. They went down the steps and into the police car.

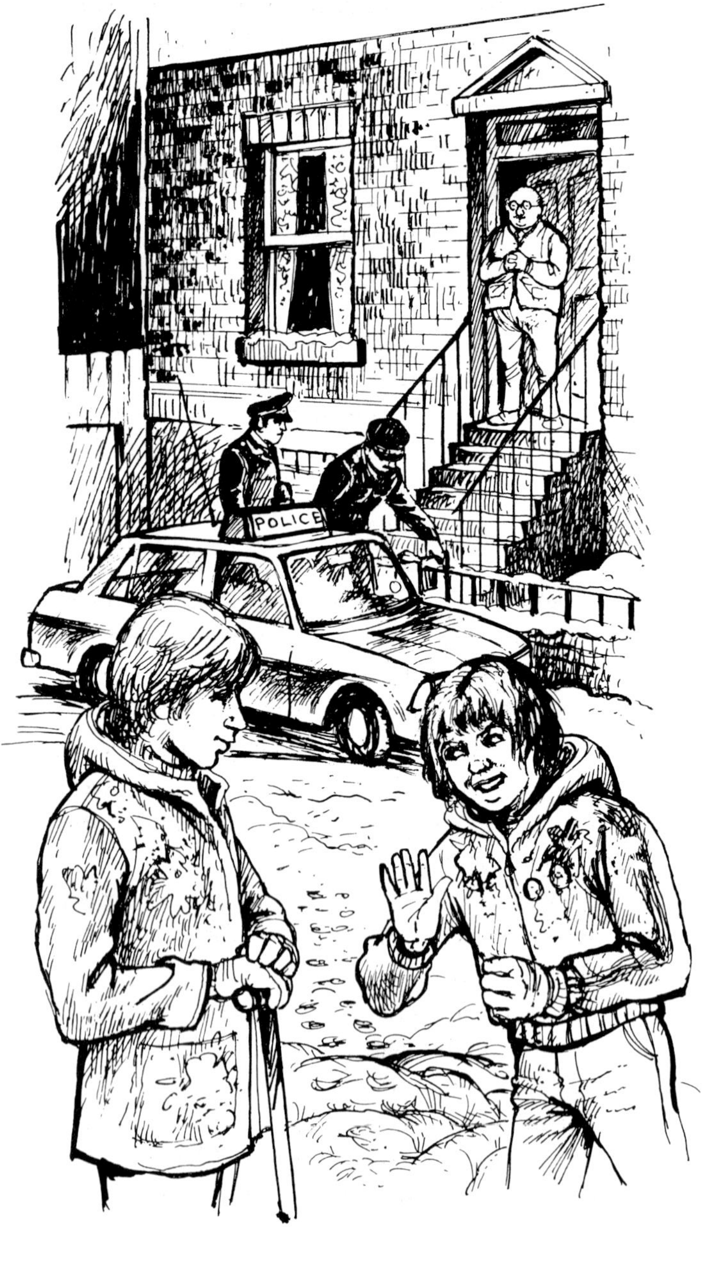
POLICE

Mr. Berryman watched them drive away, and then he came across The Yard to the two boys.

"Hallo, Tim," he said. "I suppose you didn't see any strangers prowling around in The Yard last night?"

Tim remembered Jim and Kevin.

"What's happened, Mr. Berryman?" he asked.

"Someone broke into my house last night," said Mr. Berryman. "Two of them, the police think. They stole some money, and my radio. But worst of all, they took my mother's silver spoons. I don't mind so much about the money, but I wish they hadn't taken the spoons. I'd buy them back from them, if I could. My mother was so proud of them. She would have been over a hundred, if she'd been alive today. But I'm sure she'd still be polishing those spoons."

"I'm sorry, Mr. Berryman," said Tim.

"There have been a lot of burglaries about lately," said Mr. Berryman. "The police were telling me that they've had more than ever, this last month or two.

"Well, you tell your aunt to keep her door locked. You never know who's about."

He went back to his house.

"Why didn't you tell him about those two boys we saw last night?" asked Simon. "They came into The Yard."

"How could I?" said Tim. "If I'd told him, I'd have to tell the police, too. And then they'd want to know when we saw them, and where we were, and all that. We can't say we were with the Hidden People. They'd never believe us."

Tim sounded very unhappy. He liked Mr. Berryman, and he wanted to help him.

"I'll bet it was those two," said Simon. "I wish we knew who they were."

"I do know," said Tim. "They're called Jim and Kevin. Jim's the big one. I think he's been in trouble with the police before."

"I think I've seen the younger one before," said Simon. "He stopped Jessica once, when she was coming back from the shop. He tried to take some sausage rolls she'd bought. Sebastian dropped a big stone from the top of the wall. He nearly hit him. I think that was the one you call Kevin."

"It sounds like him," said Tim.

"Couldn't we just tell Mr. Berryman about him?" asked Simon.

"I don't see how we can," said Tim. "No one knew that we were out last night. And Jim and Kevin would say we were telling lies. We've got no proof that we saw them at all."

"Couldn't we say we saw them from a window?" asked Simon.

"But we didn't," said Tim. "They'd soon find that out. And if we said we saw them by the canal, the police would want to know what *we* were doing out at that time of night. And then what are you going to say? You'd have to tell a lot of lies. They'd find out, and they wouldn't believe us. They might even think we'd stolen the things ourselves.

"No, we can't tell Mr. Berryman. But I'll go and see Melinda. The Hidden People might help us. If we could find out where Kevin and Jim were living, we might be able to get Mr. Berryman's spoons back."

"When will you go and see Melinda?" asked Simon.

"I'll go tonight, if Sebastian's back," said Tim. "He'll fly me there."

"Can I come, too?" asked Simon.

Mr. Berryman came out of his house, and crossed The Yard to the two boys. He was holding something in his hand that looked like a wet rag.

"This isn't your glove, is it, Simon?" he asked. "You're only wearing one."

He held it out.

"Yes, it's mine," said Simon. "I lost it. Thanks Mr. Berryman."

"I found it just by the back door of my house," said Mr. Berryman. "It was under the snow. I was shovelling the steps, and I saw it. How did it get there, Simon? It wasn't there yesterday. I'm sure of that. I was out in the back, clearing things up, before I went out for the evening. And it didn't get there this morning, because it was under the snow."

Simon looked at Mr. Berryman. He didn't say anything.

"Where were you last night, Simon?" asked Mr. Berryman.

"He was with me, Mr. Berryman," said Tim. "He was with me all the time, and I saw him home. Simon didn't break into your house. And I didn't. We wouldn't do that."

"H'm," said Mr. Berryman. "No, I believe you wouldn't, Tim. I've known you a long time. Well, I suppose you could have dropped it in The Yard, Simon. Perhaps someone else left it at my back door. That's possible. Are you sure you didn't go into my garden when you were playing?"

Simon shook his head. "I didn't, Mr. Berryman. Really I didn't," he said.

"All right," said Mr. Berryman. "You'd better take your glove and get it dried."

Simon swallowed.

"Thanks," he said.

He took the glove, and Mr. Berryman went back to his house.

"You'll have to stay at home tonight," said Tim. "If anyone found out that you weren't there, you'd be in real trouble. I'll go and see Melinda."

"All right," said Simon. "Do you think he believed me?"

"I think so," said Tim. "But he doesn't know you very well yet. We'd better make sure that you stay in for a bit."

Chapter Three

Sebastian came in at tea time, as Tim sat in the kitchen eating eggs and bacon and chips with Aunt May.

Sebastian rubbed himself against Tim's leg, and mewed loudly.

"You'd better give him some supper," said Aunt May. "He's been out all night, if you ask me. He must have been nearly frozen, in all this snow."

Tim got up, and picked up Sebastian. Sebastian's paws were very cold, but he didn't want to be stroked. He wanted his supper. He struggled out of Tim's arms, and mewed loudly.

Tim set Sebastian's plate down by the fire, and Sebastian ate his supper as if he hadn't had anything to eat for a week.

"I don't know how that cat manages to stay so thin, when he eats so much," said Aunt May. "Just look at him!"

Sebastian was certainly eating his supper in record time. When he had finished, he sat down by the fire to wash himself.

As soon as he had helped Aunt May to wash up, Tim went up to his room. Sebastian trotted up beside him.

Tim went over to the window, and looked out. It was a clear night. Down in The Yard the snow sparkled in the lamp-light.

"I want to see Melinda tonight, Sebastian," said Tim. "It's very important. Could you take me there?"

"Rrrrrr!" said Sebastian.

He rubbed himself against Tim's legs.

"Do you think it's too early to go now?" asked Tim.

Sebastian ran to the door. Tim let him out, and Sebastian ran off downstairs.

A few minutes later, he was outside the window, riding a broomstick. Tobias was sometimes in a bad mood, but Sebastian was always ready for anything. He was always so cheerful about it too.

Tim checked that he was wearing his magic silver coin. He put on his anorak and his gloves, and climbed on to the window sill. He looked down. There was no one in The Yard below, and no one watching from the windows of the houses.

Tim slid on to the broomstick.

"All right, Sebastian. Off we go," he said.

Sebastian waved his tail, and the broomstick climbed steeply upwards, over the roofs of the houses.

It was clear that Sebastian was going to fly very high. Tim thought that was wise of him. It was much earlier than usual for one of their journeys. There were still people about in the streets below.

They left the town behind them. Tim saw the lights of cars on the road, and the dark line of the canal below them. The fields were still white with snow.

They left Hollow Hill behind them. At last, Tim saw Piper's Wood ahead. The broomstick was coming down. There was the little bridge over the canal, and the lane, and Melinda's cottage.

Sebastian took the broomstick right up to Melinda's front door, and held it steady.

Tim got off. Sebastian jumped off, and the broomstick dropped to the ground.

There was a light on in the cottage. Tim hoped that Melinda was there alone. She hadn't asked him to come to her cottage this time and he felt a little nervous.

The face on the brass knocker looked at him even more sourly than usual. Tim never used the knocker. He picked up a stone.

He was just going to knock on the door, when it opened. Melinda stood there in the light of the doorway, looking out. Her white hair hung loose over her red shawl, as it always did. She looked stern, and rather fierce. But when she saw Tim, she smiled, and her whole face changed.

"Tim!" she said, in a pleased way. "Tim! I'm glad to see you. Come in."

She stood to one side, and Tim went in, with Sebastian at his heels.

A bright fire was burning on the hearth. It shone on the glass bottles on the shelves, on the chairs, and the tiger-skin rug in front of the fire.

"Sit down, Tim," said Melinda. "You must be cold. Sit down by the fire, and tell me why you've come."

Tim sat down. He took off his gloves, and held his hands out to the blaze. Sebastian jumped up on the chair beside him, and pushed his way on to Tim's knee.

Tim found it difficult to begin.

"It's — there's a bit of trouble in The Yard," Tim said.

"Trouble with some of the Hidden People?" asked Melinda.

"No, no," said Tim. "It's nothing like that. But someone's stolen Mr. Berryman's silver spoons. I think I know who the burglars are. But I can't tell anyone, because we were out with Captain Jory when we saw them. I — I don't know if I ought to ask you to help us, when it's not really about the Hidden People. But I don't know what to do."

"You can always ask the Hidden People for help, Tim," said Melinda. "You've helped them. They'll help you. Tell me about it."

Tim felt better. It was always much easier to talk to Melinda than he thought it would be. He told her how they had seen Kevin and Jim go into The Yard the night before.

"Kevin's the one who pushed you into the pool by the whispering trees, isn't he?" asked Melinda.

Tim nodded.

"And you think they stole Mr. Berryman's things?"

"They must have done," said Tim. "We saw them just before the snow came. They were in The Yard at the time the things were stolen. There were no footmarks in the snow this morning. No one can have gone to Mr. Berryman's house after it snowed."

"What do you want me to do?" asked Melinda.

"I wondered if the Hidden People would help me to find out where Jim and Kevin are living," said Tim. "Then I might go there and try and get the things back. The silver spoons belonged to Mr. Berryman's mother. I've got to get them back for him if I can."

"Supposing Jim and Kevin caught you?" said Melinda.

"I thought you might make me invisible," said Tim. "I'd be all right then."

Melinda smiled.

"So you would," she said.

She stared into the fire.

Tim waited, watching her face. He felt much happier now. He settled back in his chair.

"Does Tobias know Jim or Kevin?" Melinda asked at last.

Tim shook his head. "I think Sebastian might

know Kevin," he said. "Simon said that Sebastian saw him once. Kevin tried to take some sausage rolls Jessica had bought, and Sebastian dropped a stone off the wall near him."

Sebastian purred loudly. Melinda smiled.

"So Sebastian will remember him," she said. "I'll tell Tobias about all this, Tim. I'll ask him to help to look for the two of them. Tobias and Sebastian can search the town for them at night. If they've burgled one house, they'll burgle another. Tobias and Sebastian will find them for you.

"Make sure you're wearing your silver coin, day and night, so that you'll be able to see Tobias."

"Could Tobias make me invisible, too?" asked Tim. "Then I could go with him to get the spoons."

"He could if he's with you," said Melinda. "But I'll give you the magic drink which I gave you when you went north with Nicola and Jeremy. Then you could make yourself invisible if you were on your own, or with Sebastian."

"Can I give it to Arun? Or to Simon and Jessica?" asked Tim.

"If you have to," said Melinda. "But be careful with it."

She went to a cupboard in the corner of the room, and took out a little glass bottle. It had a golden top, and it was full of something that looked like red fire.

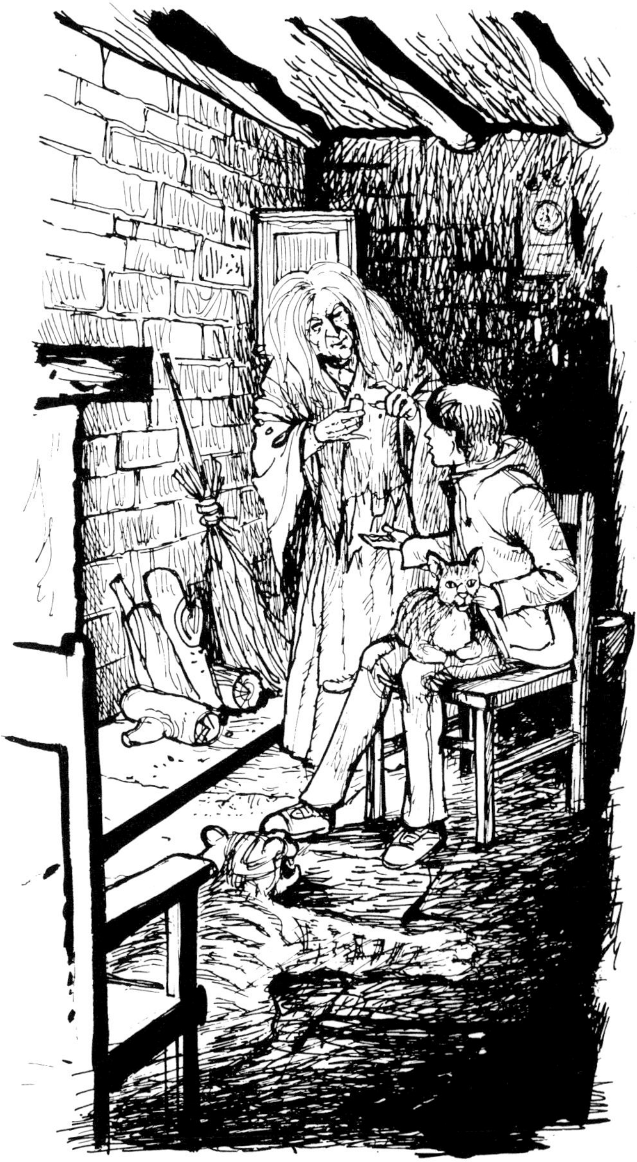

"This is another bottle of the drink which I gave you before," she said. "You remember the dose? One drop will make you invisible for an hour. Ordinary Folk won't be able to see you at all. The Hidden People will be able to see you, of course. So will anyone wearing a magic token — or one of the Strange Ones. But you'll be invisible to Ordinary Folk."

"Thank you very much," said Tim.

He took the bottle, and made sure that the cap was on tightly. Then he put it in his pocket.

"This will help a lot," he said.

"Be careful, all the same," said Melinda. "Ordinary Folk will still be able to hear you, you know. And they can shut you in. You can't walk through a door when you're invisible, any more than you can now. You're one of the Ordinary Folk. Nothing changes that."

"I ought to be able to get in and get Mr. Berryman's spoons, if Jim and Kevin have got them," said Tim. "I'd better go back now. I've got to go to school tomorrow."

He got up.

"Come and see me again if you need me, Tim," said Melinda. "Tobias will tell me what is happening."

"I'll come," said Tim. "And thank you *very* much."

Melinda opened the door for him, and he went out into the night. Sebastian ran past him, and jumped on to the end of the broomstick. The broomstick floated in the air. Tim sat on it.

"Goodnight," said Melinda.

Tim hadn't time to say anything in reply, because the broomstick took off with such a jerk that he nearly fell off. Sebastian always did fly a broomstick rather wildly. They shot up high into the air, and flew quickly towards the town.

Tim was glad when at last they swept in over the roofs of the houses in The Yard, and stopped outside his bedroom window. He climbed in first. Sebastian rode the broomstick in behind him, and dropped it on the floor. Tim pushed it under his bed.

He took out Melinda's bottle, and hid it at the back of his drawer, under his clothes. Then he got undressed and climbed into bed as quickly as he could.

Sebastian settled down at his feet, purring loudly. Tim snuggled down under the blankets. He was still worried, but he felt much better, now that he had seen Melinda. There was at least a chance that he could get the spoons back for Mr. Berryman. He pushed it all out of his mind, and went to sleep.

Chapter Four

Tim told Simon about his visit to Melinda on the way to school, the next morning.

"You'll let me come with you, won't you?" said Simon. "We'll go looking for Jim and Kevin. We could make ourselves invisible and go anywhere."

"I think we'd better let Tobias and Sebastian find out where they're staying first," said Tim. "Then I can get into the house and get the spoons."

"But I'll come too," said Simon.

"I don't think you should," said Tim. "It won't be easy, even for one. The more of us there are about, the easier it will be to get into trouble."

"But I want to be invisible," said Simon.

"I'll tell you what," said Tim. "I think I'll have to be the one to get the spoons. But when it's all over, we'll use a drop or two of Melinda's mixture, and make ourselves invisible for an hour. Just for fun."

"I'd still like to come with you, when you're looking for the spoons," said Simon. "You might meet the thieves."

"They won't be able to see me if I do," said Tim. "But I may need you. Still, I can't promise anything."

Tim met Arun at school. (Arun lived in The Yard, too, and knew the Hidden People.) They went off to a corner of the playground, and Tim told Arun what had happened at the weekend.

"I haven't been home yet," said Arun. "I stayed at my grandfather's house last night. But even my grandfather was saying that there have been a lot of burglaries lately. I wonder if that's just chance, or if it's Jim and Kevin? You'll let me help, Tim?"

"Yes, of course," said Tim. "But I don't know what we're going to have to do yet. I don't think we can do much during the week. I wish it was Easter. We can't be out all night with the Hidden People, when we have to be at school all day."

"We'll have to do things at the weekend," said Arun. "Perhaps Tobias and Sebastian will have found something out by then."

* * *

It was Friday night, before anything more happened.

During the week, Sebastian was out most of the time, and Tim guessed that he must be with Tobias. Tim scarcely saw him. Sebastian usually managed to be home for supper, but he went out again as soon as he had finished. Tim woke up once or twice, to find Sebastian asleep on his bed. But the little cat was gone by morning.

Even Aunt May noticed that Sebastian was usually missing.

"I can't think what's got into that cat," she said. "He must be courting."

"I don't think he is," said Tim.

"I shouldn't be surprised," said Aunt May.

On Friday, Tim went to bed early. He had been worrying about Mr. Berryman's spoons most of the week, and he hadn't been sleeping very well. But on Friday he fell asleep as soon as he got into bed.

He had been asleep for some hours, when the window suddenly fell open with a bang.

Tim sat up.

Tobias was standing on the foot of his bed.

"Hallo, Tim," said Tobias. "I've found them — Jim and Kevin."

"That's great, Tobias," said Tim. "Where are they?"

"They're not far away," said Tobias. "They're in a house in Bargeman's Square, on the other side of the canal. And Mr. Berryman's house isn't the only one they've burgled. I saw them climbing out of a window in Baker's Lane tonight, and followed them home. The house is full of stuff they've stolen."

"Did you see the spoons?" asked Tim.

"Yes," said Tobias. "At least, I saw *some* spoons. They've boxes of 'em. Do you know which are Mr. Berryman's?"

"I've seen them," said Tim. "I think I'd know."

"Then you'd better come with me now, and get them," said Tobias. "It shouldn't be too difficult. I'll make you invisible. Come on."

"Where's Sebastian?" asked Tim, as he scrambled out of bed.

"Melinda wanted to see him," said Tobias.

"He's taken a broomstick over to her cottage. He spotted Kevin. He was quite sure about him."

Tim pulled his clothes on over his pyjamas. He put on his gloves and his anorak. He picked up his torch, and went to the window. A broomstick was riding in the air outside.

Tobias jumped up on to the window sill, and outside on to the broomstick.

Tim pushed his torch into his pocket, and climbed out on to the broomstick himself. He had done that so many times, that he no longer thought about the drop to The Yard below.

Tobias flew the broomstick up smoothly over the roofs of the houses, and across the canal. He flew along Bridge Street, till he came to Bargeman's Square.

"That's it," he said. "That's where Jim and Kevin are."

Bargeman's Square wasn't very big. There were terraced houses on each side of it, and a grimy statue of a seaman in the middle. All the houses had basement windows, set in a well and level with the ground. Four roads ran into the square.

The house Tobias meant was at the end of a row on the far side. He flew the broomstick over to it. There was no attic window, but there was a skylight in the roof.

"They keep the stuff in the basement," said Tobias. "I've been in. But this is the best way to get inside. There are bars over the basement window, and somebody may be sleeping in the bedrooms. Shall I come down on the roof?"

"All right," said Tim.

Tobias brought the broomstick close to the skylight.

"The window's only on a catch," said Tobias. "I can move the catch back for you, and the window will open."

He twitched his tail.

Tim heard a faint click. The skylight lifted up a little way off the roof.

Tim bent down and raised it up. To his surprise, there was a ladder up to the skylight, fixed against the wall inside.

He climbed in, and stood on the ladder, holding the window up.

"What are you going to do with the broomstick?" he asked.

"Leave it in the gutter, till we come back," said Tobias. "Wait a moment."

He flew the broomstick down to the gutter, and set it down carefully. Then he ran up the tiles to the window, and jumped in on to Tim's shoulder.

"Shut the skylight carefully," he said. "We don't want to make a noise. I think they've gone to bed."

Tim shut the skylight down softly, and climbed down the ladder. It was very dark.

He pulled out his torch, and switched it on.

He was standing in a little boxroom. Old trunks and suitcases stood on each side. The boxroom had a ceiling which sloped at one side. At the top of the ladder, opposite the skylight,

Tim saw an opening in under the ridge of the roof. At the bottom of the ladder, just in front of him there was a door into the house.

Tim switched off his torch, and opened the door. When his eyes were used to the dark again, he could just make out one door to his right, and another to his left. Some railings guarded the stairwell near him.

He went out on to the landing, and closed the door behind him. He could hear someone snoring in the room to his left.

He tiptoed to the top of the stairs. There was another door there. He crept past it, and down the stairs. Tobias led the way.

"Along the passage," whispered Tobias. "This way."

He turned right at the foot of the stairs into a narrow passage, which led to an outside door.

Tim switched on his torch, and followed him. He couldn't see a black cat properly in the dark.

47

Tobias only went a few metres before he stopped in front of a door that led in under the stairs.

Tim opened it, and saw a flight of steps leading down into a cellar.

"This way," said Tobias. "Everything's down here."

He ran down the steps, and Tim followed.

There was a pile of coal in front of him, near the foot of the stairs. There was another door on the right.

"It's all in there," said Tobias softly, looking at the door.

Tim turned the handle. The door opened. He went in with Tobias, and shut the door softly behind him.

Tim lifted his torch, and shone the beam first on one side of the room, and then on the other.

The room was like Aladdin's cave. There was a red curtain across the window. There were shelves all round the walls, and a table in the middle of the room. The light from the torch picked up the sparkle of silver. There were silver mugs and trays; silver teapots and jugs; candlesticks and vases. There were open boxes of silver spoons, and other boxes with silver knives and forks in them.

Tim drew in a deep breath.

One shelf was packed with radios and cassette players, and flat closed boxes. Tim guessed that the boxes held more spoons and cutlery. But when he opened one, he found that it was full of necklaces and rings, which sparkled in the light.

"They must have been stealing things for weeks!" Tim said.

"Months, I should think," said Tobias. "Can you see the spoons you want anywhere?"

"They'll be in one of these boxes, I expect," said Tim. "Yes, this looks like it."

He was just putting out his hand to pick up one of the flat boxes, when a big rat suddenly leapt out from behind a box on the shelf, and scuttled down on to the floor.

Tim was so startled that he jumped backwards. He tripped over some fire-irons which were propped up against the table.

The fire-irons fell to the ground with a crash. Tim turned quickly. He knocked against an open box of cutlery, and that, too, crashed to the ground.

"Quick," said Tobias. "They'll have heard us. Have you got Mr. Berryman's spoons?"

Tim picked up the flat box. He opened it, and shone his torch on it.

"This is it," he said. "I remember it. I'm sure this is the one."

"Good," said Tobias. "Put it under your sweater. You're invisible now. If it's under your sweater, it will be invisible, too. There's someone coming."

Tim pushed the box up under his sweater, and moved to the far corner of the room. He stood there, scarcely daring to breathe.

He listened. Tobias' ears were a good deal sharper than his, for at first he heard nothing. But then there were footsteps overhead. A door opened, and he heard the footsteps coming down the flight of stairs to the basement.

"The door's shut," said Kevin's voice, outside.

"Open it, then," he heard a man say. "We'll soon see what's happening."

The door was flung open. Someone switched on the light.

A big man was standing in the doorway. Tim stared at his hand. He was holding a gun. The big man was wearing pyjamas. He had thick black hair. His face was rather pale, as though he wasn't often out in the sun, and he had a black beard.

"There's no one here," he said, stepping in and looking round.

Tim held his breath. The man was looking straight at him.

"A box has fallen down," said Kevin, coming into the room behind him. "And the fire-irons."

The rat suddenly shot out from behind a box, streaked across the room, and ran out of the door.

The big man laughed and Tim breathed again.

"That's what it was," he said. "Just a rat. What a racket it made! I must get some traps in the morning. I'm surprised it didn't wake Jim up."

"He's tired," said Kevin. "We'd only just got to bed. We did that house in Baker's Lane tonight."

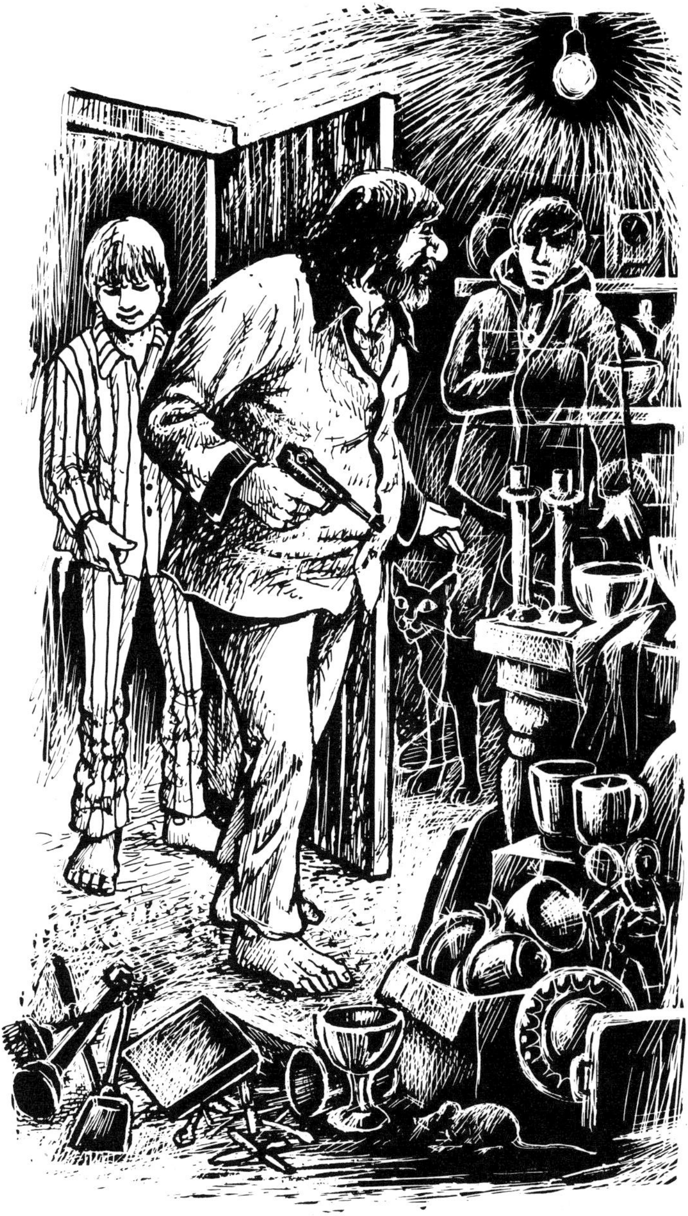

"Get anything?" asked the man. He glanced round the room. "I don't see anything new."

"We just got some money," said Kevin.

"How much?" asked the man.

"Five pounds," said Kevin.

"Five pounds!" exclaimed the man. "Five pounds! You do a house, and you only get five pounds! Wasn't there anything else you could take?"

"She woke up," said Kevin. "That old woman, Mrs. Kelsey."

"So what happened?" asked the man. Suddenly, he sounded very angry.

"She came down and found us. Jim thumped her."

"Well — what happened then? You'd better tell me, Kevin."

He glared angrily at Kevin. Kevin took a step backwards.

"It wasn't me," he said. "It was Jim. And he didn't hit her very hard."

"You don't have to, when they're that age," said the man. "How old is she? Eighty? Well — what happened?"

"She fell over, and we left," said Kevin sulkily.

"You ran away, you mean," said the man. "You fools! You stupid fools! Don't you know that you could kill an old woman like that? And then where would you be?"

"Jim only pushed her over," said Kevin. "She was breathing all right."

"Well, I hope she still is," said the man.

52

"You stupid fools! I've told you not to use violence. I won't have people using violence, when they're working for me. You may be my nephews, but you're working for me, just the same."

"You've got a gun, yourself," said Kevin.

"So I've got a gun!" growled the big man. "All right. I keep it in this house. *In this house,* Kevin. I don't take it out with me, when I do a job. There's a lot of stuff in this house just now. I keep a gun here to protect it — against any of our friends who might fancy it. But I don't take it out with me. Not me. I'm not a fool.

"Did anyone see you and Jim in Baker's Lane?"

"I — I think they might have done," said Kevin. "There was an old man in the street when we got out of the window. He shouted at us. And then he went to the house. He was knocking on the door when we ran round the corner."

"And you didn't tell me!" exclaimed the big man. "You just came home and went to bed! And Jim went to sleep! You're even more stupid than I thought.

"Well, at least that man will have got help — called the police, I expect. So the old woman will be looked after. I hope she doesn't die, that's all."

"People don't die when they just fall over," said Kevin.

"They do sometimes, if they're over eighty," said the big man. "Old bones break easily. I hope she's all right, for your sake. I'll send you both out of town tomorrow. You can stay at Piper's Farm for a time, till this has blown over.

"You'd better get to bed now. I'll have something to say to Jim in the morning!"

The big man switched off the light. They went out, shutting the door behind them. Tim heard the key turn in the lock. Footsteps went back up the stairs. The door at the top of the steps closed. They heard footsteps overhead, and then the house was quiet again.

"We're locked in," said Tim quietly, switching on his torch.

"Don't let that worry you," said Tobias. "I can manage a simple lock like that. Let's just give them time to get back to bed. Put the torch out. We don't want anyone outside to see a torch flashing down here."

They waited silently in the darkness. Tim could feel his heart beating. It was all very well for Tobias to be so certain that he could get out. Tim wasn't at all sure.

It seemed a long time to Tim, before Tobias said: "I think they'll be asleep now. Come on. I'll turn that lock back."

Tim couldn't see what Tobias did. (Tobias was difficult to see in the dark.) But he heard the lock click back.

"Open the door," said Tobias. "We can go now."

Tim groped his way across to the door, and turned the handle. The door opened. Tim breathed a sigh of relief. He went through it into the darkness of the cellar.

"Tobias?" he whispered.

"I'm here, Tim," said Tobias. "Shut the door."

Tim closed the door very quietly.

"You can switch that torch on now, if you want to," said Tobias. "I suppose *you* can't see in the dark. It must be very difficult, being one of the Ordinary Folk."

"It's easier when you have one of the Hidden People with you," Tim said.

Tobias stood for a moment, facing the door. His long tail stretched out behind him. His ears went back.

The lock on the door clicked shut.

"That'll fool them," he said. "Come on, Tim. Let's get away."

He led the way up the stairs. Tim opened the door at the top, and they went out into the hall.

"He keeps the key in the drawer of that little table," whispered Tobias. "I saw him get it out, last time I was in the house. So it's there if you want it. Switch your torch out now."

Tim saw the little table. He switched his torch off, and groped his way to the stairs.

When he got to the landing above, he stood still for a moment, listening. He heard snores coming from the back room.

Tobias laughed softly.

"They're asleep again," he whispered. "Come on."

Tim tiptoed along the landing, and went into the boxroom. In the light that filtered in through the skylight, he saw Tobias already standing on the top of the ladder.

"You'd better open the skylight, Tim," said Tobias. "It bangs a bit, if I do it."

Tim climbed up the ladder. He undid the catch, and pushed up the skylight. Tobias jumped out on to the roof, and Tim climbed after him.

"Wait here while I get the broomstick," said Tobias. "Ordinary Folk are no good at climbing roofs."

Tim hung on to the edge of the open skylight.

Tobias went quickly down the roof to the gutter. Tim saw him twitch his tail. The broomstick lifted into the air. Tobias jumped on one end, and rode it back up to the skylight.

Tim moved on to it carefully. He held on to the broomstick with one hand, and shut the skylight with the other. It slipped, and came down with a bang.

Tobias flicked his tail, and the broomstick shot up and over the roof.

"I thought you could close it *quietly*," he said over his shoulder. "I couldn't have made a bigger bang myself. Not that it matters. They won't know what's happened. You've still got the spoons safely?"

Tim touched the hard box under his sweater.

"Yes," he said.

"Then there's nothing to worry about," said Tobias.

"Yes, there is," said Tim. "Do you think we could go over to Baker's Lane before we go home? I'd like to be sure someone *did* help the old lady who lives there."

"All right," said Tobias. "But we shouldn't be too long. It will be getting light soon. You don't want someone to go up to your room and find you out. Not after what's been happening."

He swung the broomstick back over Bargeman's Square, and across the roofs of the houses on the far side.

In a few minutes, Tim saw Baker's Lane below them. The street lights were on, and so were all the lights in one of the houses. An ambulance was standing outside the door, and there was a police car in the road.

As they flew over, the front door opened, and two men carried a stretcher out to the ambulance.

"There you are," said Tobias. "That man must have called the police. There's nothing more you can do."

"All right," said Tim. "Let's get home."

He was shivering a little. He wasn't sure whether it was because he was cold, or whether it was because he felt so troubled about the old lady.

Tobias swept the broomstick round in a big circle, and headed for The Yard.

They flew over the canal and through the gap in the houses. The broomstick stopped outside Tim's window.

"Here we are, Tim," said Tobias. "You can take the spoons back to Mr. Berryman's yourself, can't you? You've got some of Melinda's magic drink with you?"

"I've got it in my room," said Tim. "Yes, I'll be all right — at least, I think I will."

"Make sure you take the silver whistle with you," said Tobias. "The one Melinda gave you. Then you can call Sebastian, if you get into trouble."

Melinda had given Tim a silver whistle. He couldn't hear it himself when he blew it, but Sebastian could, even if he was a long way away. The whistle was in Tim's drawer.

"I'll take it," Tim said. "Thanks, Tobias. I'll be all right now."

He climbed into his bedroom.

"Goodnight," said Tobias.

He was gone before Tim could reply.

Tim shut the window, and lit the candle by

his bed. He pulled the box of silver spoons out from under his sweater, and opened it. Yes. He was sure that those were the ones Mr. Berryman had shown him.

He pushed the box into his top drawer behind his clothes. Then he undressed, and got into bed.

"I'll have to do something about it," he said to himself. "I can't let Kevin and Jim go on like this. I'll have to try and stop them. We all will. I'll tell Arun in the morning."

He suddenly felt very tired. There was nothing more he could do that night. It was nearly morning anyway.

Tim shut his eyes, and went to sleep.

Chapter Five

"Tim! Tim! Are you awake? TIM!"

Tim opened his eyes and sat up.

The sunlight was streaming into his room. Aunt May was calling up the attic stairs.

"I'm coming," he called back.

"Be quick. I want you down here straight away," called Aunt May.

Tim jumped out of bed. Aunt May didn't often speak like that. It must be something important. He put on his clothes as quickly as he could. He pulled a comb through his hair, and ran downstairs.

Aunt May was in the kitchen, down in the basement. There were two policemen with her. Tim could see that Aunt May was very upset.

"Did you go out last night, Tim?" she asked, as he came into the room.

"Just for a bit," said Tim.

"Where did you go, Tim?" asked one of the policemen.

"Over to Bargeman's Square," said Tim.

"Did you go into Baker's Lane?"

Tim shook his head. "No," he said.

It was quite true. He hadn't gone *into* Baker's Lane. He'd flown over it on the broomstick.

"Are you sure?" asked the policeman.

"Yes," said Tim.

"What time was it when you went out?"

"I don't know," said Tim. "I wasn't out very long. I was in most of the evening."

60

"What did you do?" asked the policeman.

"Nothing much."

"Why did you go? You must have gone over there for some reason?"

Tim thought hard. He didn't want to tell any lies, but he couldn't tell them about Tobias and the silver spoons.

"I was looking for the burglars," he said at last. "Mr. Berryman is upset about losing his things. I wanted to help him to get them back."

"H'm," said the policeman. "You can leave that to us, Tim. Are you sure you didn't take anything from Mr. Berryman's house yourself the other night?"

"Of course I didn't," said Tim. He turned to Aunt May. "You know I wouldn't," he said. "Mr. Berryman's a friend of mine."

"I know he is, Tim," said Aunt May. "But they say that they found a muddy footprint inside Mr. Berryman's. And it was made by a boy's shoe, not a man's. And there was another one just like it in the house in Baker's Lane."

"Well, it wasn't mine," said Tim.

"Your foot's about the right size," said the policeman. "And it was your kind of shoe."

"Lots of boys wear shoes like that. And girls too!" said Aunt May.

"So they do," said the policeman. "Well, Tim, here's something else. You said that young Simon was with you, the night Mr. Berryman's house was burgled, didn't you?"

"He *was* with me," said Tim. "He was with me all evening."

61

"Mr. Berryman found Simon's glove just outside his back window, next morning," said the policeman.

"Simon didn't go into Mr. Berryman's house," said Tim. "Not when he was with me. And I'm sure he didn't go in afterwards."

"Why are you so sure?" asked the policeman.

"He wouldn't do it," said Tim.

"H'm," the policeman said again. He turned to Aunt May. "Could we go up to Tim's room?" he asked. "Would you mind if we took a quick look through his things?"

Tim drew in a quick breath. He couldn't help himself. He thought of the drawer, with his clothes in it. Mr. Berryman's silver spoons were in that drawer. So was the silver whistle, and Melinda's bottle with the magic drink.

The policeman looked at him quickly.

"What's wrong with our looking in your room, Tim?" he asked.

"Nothing," said Tim.

"You're looking a bit pale," said the policeman.

"Anyone would look pale, with policemen in the house," said Aunt May. "You don't mind, do you, Tim? We'll all go upstairs together. Come along."

Aunt May led the way up to Tim's attic bedroom. Tim followed her, and both policemen came up after them.

Tim thought that he had never been so unhappy in all his life. They would find the spoons, and then everyone would think he'd taken them. Mr. Berryman wouldn't be friends with him any longer. He would think Tim was a thief. And Aunt May — how would Aunt May feel? But there was nothing he could do about it.

He stood at one side, while the policemen went quickly over the room, looking at everything.

"I'll just look in the drawers," one of them said, turning to Aunt May.

"You can look anywhere you like," said Aunt May. "Tim's got nothing to hide, have you, Tim?"

Tim said nothing. He wished that Aunt May was right.

The policeman opened the top drawer, and pushed Tim's clothes to one side.

Tim held his breath.

The policeman felt in the back of the drawer. He felt all around among the clothes. He pulled out his hand and shut the drawer. He opened the lower drawers, and looked in them, too.

"Nothing here," he said to the other policeman.

Tim stared at him. He could scarcely believe his ears.

"I'll just take a quick look in the other attic," said the other policeman. He went across the landing.

"We'll wait for you downstairs," said Aunt May. "Come along, Tim."

They went downstairs to the kitchen in silence. One policeman went with them.

The second one soon joined them. Tim saw him look at the first policeman and shake his head.

"Well, that's all right so far," said the first policeman. "You keep it that way, Tim. Stay at home at night. Don't go out looking for burglars. Leave that to the police. Good morning, Miss McNair. Thanks very much."

"I'll see you out," said Aunt May.

She went upstairs with the two men to the

front door. Tim sat down on a chair. His knees were shaking so much that he could scarcely stand.

Aunt May came bustling down the stairs again.

"Well, that's over," she said. "You do look a bit white, Tim. You've no need to be afraid of policemen. They're people who help you, really — unless you've done anything wrong. They had me worried for a bit. I didn't like the way they looked at you. But I knew you wouldn't do anything like that. I know you, Tim."

She came over to him, and gave him a hug.

Tim was surprised. Aunt May didn't often hug him. In fact, she'd been very good about everything. He had felt that she was defending him. She was on his side.

"I'm glad they've gone," he said.

"Have your breakfast, and you'll feel better," said Aunt May. "You do look white. What did you want to go out at night for, looking for burglars? You'll never find them — and I'd rather you didn't. I don't want you to get into trouble — and I don't want you to get hurt."

"I'll be all right," said Tim.

"Well, you stay at home and get your rest," said Aunt May. "I can't go out myself, if I think you're wandering about. And I have to go and work at the shop. We need the money.

"Here's your breakfast. Eat that, and you'll feel better."

Tim ate his breakfast. It did make him feel

rather better. But he thought that he would feel better still, when he had looked in his drawers. He was so thankful that the spoons hadn't been found. He choked over his tea, at the thought of what might have happened.

Tim got out of the kitchen as soon as he could, and raced upstairs two steps at a time. He opened the door of his room, ran over to the chest of drawers, and pulled open the top drawer.

He pushed his clothes on one side. The policeman was right. There was nothing but his clothes in the drawer. The spoons, the whistle, and Melinda's bottle had all gone.

"Is this what you're looking for?" said a voice behind him.

Tim spun round.

A boy of about his own age was standing in the doorway. He was dressed in a strange looking coat and knee breeches. He had black shoes, with brass buckles, on his feet. He was holding the box of spoons, the whistle and the bottle in his hands.

"Jared!" cried Tim. "Jared! However did you get here?"

He had last seen Jared by the fire on Hollow Hill.

Jared laughed.

"Sebastian brought me," he said. "He's outside, putting the broomstick away. We were talking to Jessica, when we heard the police car drive into The Yard. We saw it stop outside your house, and Jessica thought you might need some help. So Sebastian flew me over."

"I'm so glad!" cried Tim. "I thought I'd had it, that time!"

He laughed shakily. He still hadn't quite got over the anxiety of the last hour.

"Where were you, when the police were up here?" he asked.

"I was in the back attic, but they couldn't see me, of course," said Jared. "And I hid your things under my coat, so they couldn't see them, either. Here's Sebastian."

Sebastian came running up the stairs. He dashed in, and took a flying leap into Tim's arms. He was purring loudly.

"Sebastian's very pleased with himself," said Jared.

"I'm pleased with him, too," said Tim. "And with you. I can't tell you how thankful I am that you were here."

"Melinda told me what was happening," said Jared, "and I thought I'd come and see if I could help. But it was Jessica who guessed that the police might search your room. Shall I put the spoons back in Mr. Berryman's house for you? It's the house in the corner, isn't it?"

"Could you?" said Tim. "I'll show you which house it is."

They went to the window. Tim pointed to Mr. Berryman's house. "Look. It's that one over there."

"I'll take them over straight away," said Jared. He put the box with the spoons into an inside pocket in his coat. "You'd better take the other things."

Tim took the whistle and Melinda's bottle, and put them back in his drawer.

"Someone ought to keep a watch on the house in Bargeman's Square," he said. "Do you know about it?"

Jared nodded.

"Tobias told me about it," he said. "He came back just before I left. Would you like me to go along there after I've taken the spoons back?"

"Could you go and take a look?" asked Tim. "I don't expect they'll move anything during the day, but you never know. We'll need to know where they hide their loot. But come back this afternoon. We'll have to have a meeting with the others. We've got to stop Jim and Kevin somehow. They've really hurt someone this time. I'll get Arun. Jessica and Simon ought to be there, too."

"All right," said Jared. "I'll go now. I'll walk. Then Sebastian can stay with you and get some sleep. He's tired."

"I'll come down with you," said Tim. "I'll go across and see Arun right away."

Chapter Six

They went down into The Yard together. Tim stopped under the tree. He watched Jared go across to Mr. Berryman's house, and round to the back garden.

He was just going across to Arun's, when Arun opened the front door and came running down the steps to join him.

"Hallo, Tim," said Arun. "Is everything all right? I saw the police car from my window. What's happened?"

"Did you see Jared?" asked Tim.

Arun shook his head.

"I haven't got the magic key on me this morning," he said. "I'll put it on right away. What happened?"

"The police came because they'd found a boy's footprint in Mr. Berryman's. And Jim and Kevin burgled another house last night, and hurt an old lady. There was a boy's footprint in that house too. Mr. Berryman told the police about finding Simon's glove in his garden. So they came to see me."

"How rotten," said Arun. "Was it all right?"

"Yes," said Tim. "But it was nearly all wrong."

"The police went over to Simon's house, after they left you," said Arun. "I was watching them. But there was no one in, so they left."

The door of Simon's house opened, and Simon and Jessica came running down the steps and across The Yard to join them.

"What's happened?" cried Simon. "What were the police doing?"

Tim told them.

"It was a good thing you sent Jared across to my room, Jess," he said. "Last night, Tobias took me along to the place where Jim and Kevin are living. We found Mr. Berryman's spoons, and I brought them back with me. They were in my drawer. Jared got there just before the police, and hid them. He's taken them over to Mr. Berryman's now."

"The police came over to us, too," said Simon. "It was after they'd left you — after Jared had gone. But Uncle Joe and Aunt Lizzie were out, so the front door was locked. And you bet we didn't open it!"

"Look here," said Tim. "We've got to have a proper meeting. We've got to stop Jim and Kevin. They're not only stealing things. They knocked an old lady down.

"They're working with their uncle. I'll tell you all about it, but it will take a bit of time. We've got to stop them somehow."

"Come over to my house this afternoon," said Arun. "Come and have some tea. Dad's away, and Mother's going out with Sita. She won't mind a bit. Then we can work it all out."

"Could we?" said Tim. "That would really help."

"Yes, of course," said Arun.

"I'll come right after dinner," said Tim. "You, too, Jess? And Simon?"

"You bet," said Simon.

"Come as soon as you can," said Arun. "Then we'll have the whole afternoon."

* * *

They all met at Arun's house at half past two. Arun took them up to his bedroom.

Like Tim, Arun slept in the attic overlooking The Yard. The room had been fitted up for him like a study. He had a table, with a drawer in it, for a desk. There were shelves for his books all along one wall. There was a carpet on the floor. He had an electric fire, too, so that the room was warm. His bed was covered with a rug, so that he could use it as a sofa. There was an armchair, another small table and a straight chair for the desk. There was a chest of drawers and a cupboard, too. The room looked bright and comfortable.

Arun sat in the straight chair. He made Tim sit in the armchair, because he said it was Tim's meeting. Jessica and Simon sat on the sofa-bed.

"Now, then," said Arun. "Tell us all about it, Tim. What's happened since we last saw you?"

Tim told them about his adventures with Tobias. He told them what Jim and Kevin had been doing, and what their uncle had said. He told them about the gun. He told them how the police had come to see him, and the questions they asked.

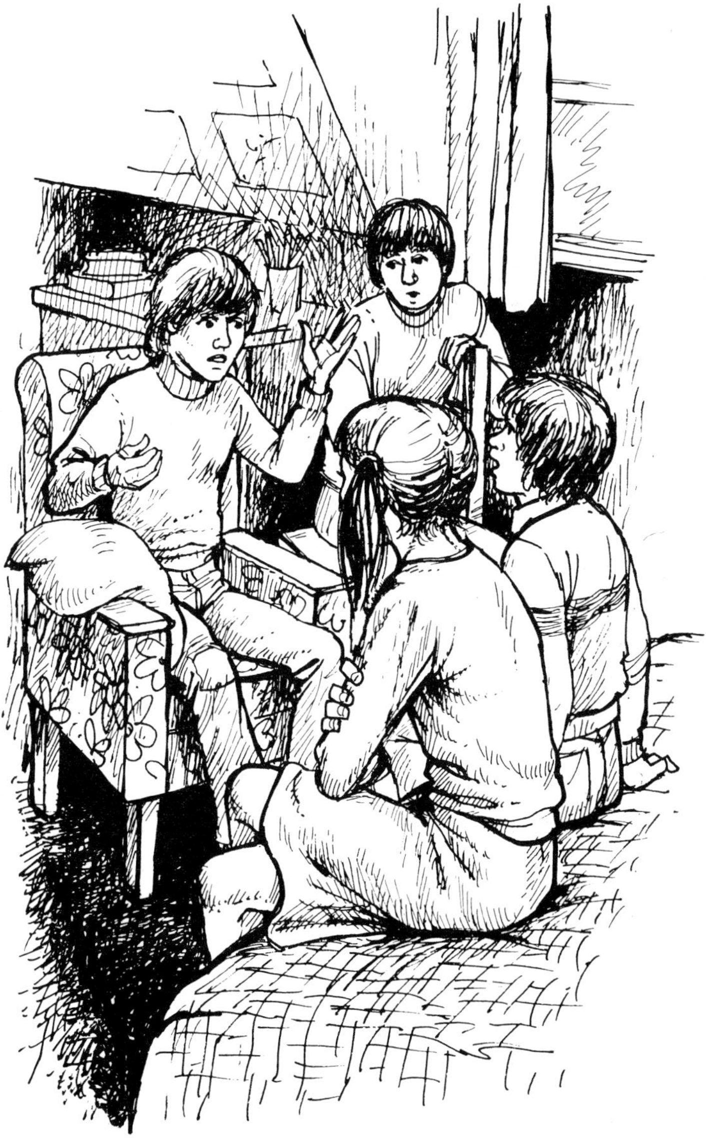

"You can see why we've got to stop Jim and Kevin," he said. "The police think we've been doing some of the burglaries. But it's not just that. Jim must have hit that old lady really hard. They took her to hospital in an ambulance. We flew over Baker's Lane, and I saw them carry her out.

"And that won't be the last time Jim hits someone. You know what he's like, Arun. We've got to stop him."

"You don't have to hit old people very hard to hurt them," said Arun. "They can break their bones, just falling over. And if they break their bones, they sometimes die."

"That's what Kevin's uncle said," said Tim.

"There's only one way to stop Jim and Kevin," said Arun. "We'll have to tell the police what we know."

"We can't do that," said Tim. "They'd want to know *how* we knew. We can't tell them about the Hidden People. They wouldn't believe us if we did. They'd think we'd been helping Jim and Kevin do the burglaries ourselves. They'd think we'd decided to shop them."

"Shop them?" questioned Simon.

"Tell the police what we knew," said Tim. "The police would think we were doing it to save ourselves."

"And then, always ever after, they'd think *we* were really burglars, too," said Jessica.

"That's just it," said Tim. "We've got to think of some way of showing the police who the real burglars are, without them knowing we're helping them."

"But how?" asked Arun. "I don't see how we can do that."

"Of course we can!" cried Jessica. "The Hidden People will help us. What we've got to do, is to see the police find a lot of clues, leading them to the real burglars! I'm sure we can do it."

"Jessica's right," said Tim. "I've been thinking about it. We've got to plant clues."

"What sort of clues?" asked Arun.

"The loot!" cried Simon cheerfully. "The police have got to find the loot."

"We've got to get them to search Jim's house, the way they did Tim's room," said Jessica. "Could we ring them up and tell them to go and look there? We needn't tell them who was ringing."

"We can't do that," said Tim. "They'd guess it was us. And either they wouldn't take any notice, or else they'd find the things, and then come and question us. That won't do. We've got to think of something else."

"I'll tell you what," said Jessica. "The police are bound to be keeping a bit of a look-out at night just now, with all the burglaries around here. Why don't we wait till they're just going by Jim's house, and then put a silver candlestick or something for them to see on the pavement? Jared could do it for us. They won't be able to see him."

"I could do it, too," said Tim. "I've got

Melinda's mixture. I can make myself invisible for an hour or two any time."

"You said I could be invisible sometime, too," said Simon.

"We all could," said Tim. "But we'll have to be careful. People can hear us, you know, even when they can't see us. It's more dangerous to go round in a crowd. Don't forget that gun.

"And there's something else. Jim and Kevin aren't in that house now. They were going to leave this morning."

"Do you know where they are?" asked Arun.

"Their uncle said they'd better go to Piper's Farm," said Tim.

"Isn't the wood near Melinda's house called Piper's Wood?" asked Jessica.

"Good for you, Jess," said Simon. "I bet Piper's Farm is near there."

"I expect you're right," said Tim. "Perhaps Jared will know."

"You could take lots of things from the house in Bargeman's Square," said Jessica. "We could use one or two, to get the police to search there. And then we could take the others to Piper's Farm, and hide them there. Sebastian would fly us there one night."

"That would do it," said Arun.

They went on discussing their plans till tea time. Arun and Jessica went downstairs to collect a couple of trays with the tea things. Arun's mother had put out two plates of little cakes and chocolate biscuits for them to eat. Arun made some toast, and took it upstairs.

Tim wandered across to the window and looked down into The Yard. Jared was standing by the old tree.

"Have you got your magic coin on, Simon?" asked Tim.

"You bet," said Simon.

"Jared's by the tree. Would you fetch him?"

"Oh, good," said Simon. He ran off down the stairs.

By the time Arun's mother came home, they had eaten their tea and worked out their plans. Nothing was to happen till the next weekend. Everyone agreed that, while they had to be at school all day, they must get some sleep at night, unless there was an emergency. But Sebastian was to be asked to keep an eye on Bargeman's Square during the week. Jared knew Piper's Farm. He would ask Tobias to watch what was happening there. In the meantime, Jared would watch the police cars at night, and see if he could find out when one was likely to drive through Bargeman's Square. When he wasn't on watch, Jared would stay with Tim. Tim and Jared would capture some of the loot next Friday night, if they could. Then they would try to put the rest of their plan into action as soon as possible.

Tim had said goodbye to the others, and was just going into his own gate, when Mr. Berryman called to him.

"Tim! Wait a moment," called Mr. Berryman.

Tim turned round. Mr. Berryman was just

coming out of his house. Tim went over to him.

"Hallo, Mr. Berryman," he said.

"Tim," said Mr. Berryman. "Tim, the most extraordinary thing has happened."

"What is it?" asked Tim.

"You remember I told you that the thieves had taken my mother's silver spoons?" asked Mr. Berryman.

Tim nodded.

"Well, someone has brought them back," said Mr. Berryman. "I went into the dining room just now, and there they were, on the table. They weren't there at dinner time."

"I'm so glad you've got them back," said Tim.

"So am I," said Mr. Berryman. "But I wish I knew how they got back, Tim."

Tim said nothing.

"I suppose you don't know anything about it?" asked Mr. Berryman.

"I've been over with Arun all the afternoon," said Tim. "Jessica and Simon were there, too."

"Well, it's a strange thing," said Mr. Berryman. "I didn't tell anyone about those spoons, except you and Simon, and the police. Of course, the police may have told other people. I expect they have. But what kind of burglar would take those spoons, and then bring them back? *You* knew that they meant a lot to me, but the burglars didn't. And they wouldn't have cared, if they *had* known, would they?"

"I didn't take your spoons, Mr. Berryman," said Tim.

Mr. Berryman sighed.

"Well, Tim, I'm glad to have them back," he said. "I hope everyone else gets their things back, too. I expect other people care as much about some of their things, as I do about my mother's spoons.

"All right, Tim. I won't ask any more questions. But I hope you're all right, boy. I do hope you're all right."

He turned, and went back into his house.

Tim went slowly indoors, and up to his room.

"We've got to fix it up next weekend," he said to himself. "We've just got to. Mr. Berryman will always think we did it, if they don't find Jim and Kevin."

Jared had gone back to Bargeman's Square. Tim wondered whether they should wait for the weekend, or put their plan into action now. But when he thought about it, he decided that it was better to wait. They had to find out when the police patrolled Bargeman's Square before they could do anything else at all.

Chapter Seven

Tim saw very little of Jared that week. Jared came up into Tim's room to sleep during the day, while Tim was at school, but he was out every night. Sebastian was usually out with him.

Jared looked after himself. Tim offered to get him something to eat, but Jared only laughed. He always said that he didn't need anything, because he had already eaten. Tim didn't know where Jared got his food.

The week seemed to go very slowly. The days dragged by.

On Thursday night, Tim went to bed as usual. He lay awake for some time, thinking over their plans. None of them felt that they could wait much longer. Friday was to be the big night. Jared was going to come with Tobias. They still hadn't quite decided what each of them was going to do, and Tim lay in bed, trying to plan out all their movements.

He was just deciding that it would be best for Jared and Tobias to go into the house in Bargeman's Square, to bring some of the stolen things out, when his window dropped open with a bang.

Tim sat up. The moon was shining in through the window. He saw a figure climb in. A cat jumped in after him.

"Jared?" questioned Tim. "Tobias?"

"Hallo, Tim," said Tobias. "Sorry to wake you up, but we had to see you."

"What's happened?" asked Tim.

"We've had a message from Melinda," said Jared. "Something's happened. I don't know what it is. It's nothing to do with you, or the burglars. It's something about witches. But Melinda wants me to go back straight away, if you can manage without me. She wants Tobias, too. She needs us."

"But you were going to help us to get the things out of the house in Bargeman's Square," said Tim.

"I know," said Jared. "But we mustn't do it tonight. They might miss the things, and guess someone was after them. You could do it yourself tomorrow. You've got Melinda's mixture. You can make yourself invisible. And Sebastian will be here to help you. We've seen him just now. He'll be here in a few minutes."

"But —" began Tim.

"I've found out about the policeman for you, Tim," said Jared. "And it's good news. There's a foot patrol, as well as a police car. A policeman walks round Bargeman's Square every night, between half-past twelve and one o'clock. At least, that's what he's done every night this week. That's much easier for you, than if there was only a police car. If you put some of the silver things on the pavement, he'll be sure to see them.

"And there's something else, Tim. I've been to Piper's Farm, and I've brought you these."

He held out a pair of training shoes.

"They belong to Kevin," he said. "I think they were the shoes he was wearing when he

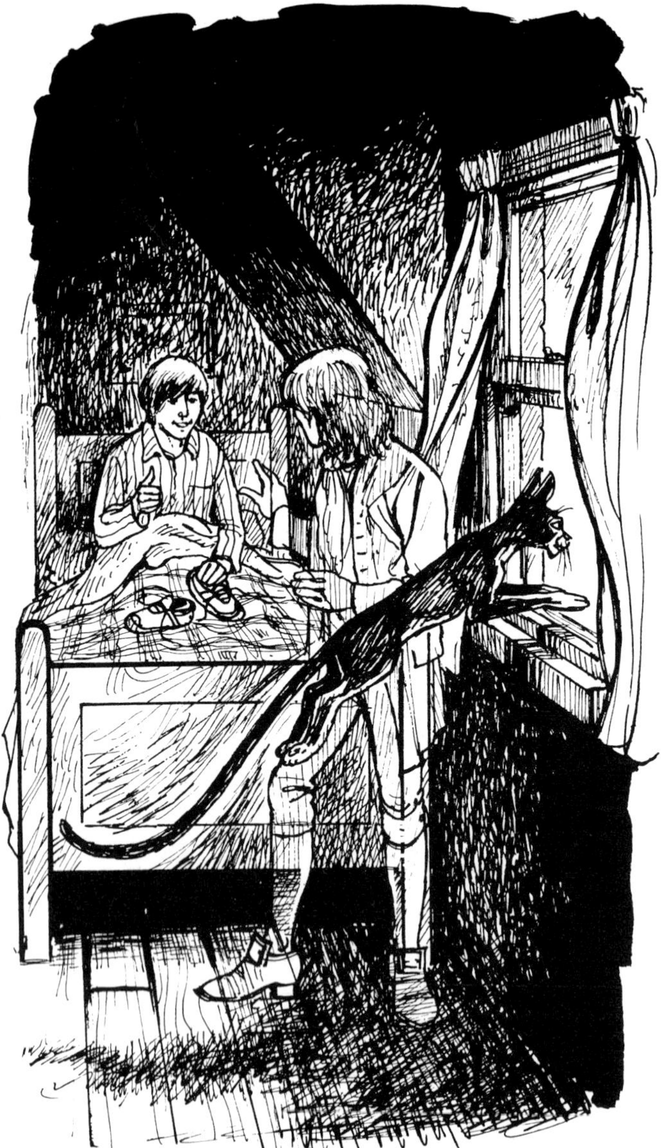

went out at night, breaking into people's houses. Put them somewhere in the house in Bargeman's Square. When they find those, the police will start looking really hard.

"I'm sorry I have to go, Tim. I really am. I wanted to be there to help. But I must go, when Melinda needs me."

Tim had said something very like that himself before now. He knew that Melinda wouldn't have called Jared back, unless she really needed him.

"All right," he said. "We'll manage. You've been a great help, anyway — finding out about that policeman, and bringing those shoes."

"Sebastian knows where Piper's Farm is," said Jared. "He'll take you there. It's not far from Piper's Wood. You won't all be able to go, because there will only be one broomstick. But two of you should be able to do everything."

"We don't want too many people trying to hide things anyway," said Tim. "We'll manage."

"I'm sorry, Tim," said Jared again.

"Don't worry," said Tim. "You have to go if Melinda needs you. I know that. And thanks for all you've done. Are you going now?"

"Yes, right away," said Jared. "We only came in to tell you. We'll come back when we can. Goodbye."

He went back to the window. Tobias jumped outside. Jared climbed out after him. Tobias must have had the broomstick waiting. Jared gave Tim a final wave, and dropped out of sight.

Tim lay back and pulled up the bedclothes. He was thinking hard. They were going to have to manage by themselves, and he must work out exactly what had to be done. He would have to go into the house in Bargeman's Square, and get the silver out himself.

He was still working out his plan, when Sebastian sailed in through the open window on a broomstick. The broomstick dropped to the floor, and Sebastian jumped on to the bed.

"Rrrrr?" questioned Sebastian.

Tim put out a hand, and Sebastian rubbed himself against it.

"You never leave me, do you, Sebastian?" said Tim. "You're the best little cat anyone ever had. But I suppose they did have to go, if Melinda needed them. Never mind. I know how we can do it ourselves."

"Rrrrr!" said Sebastian.

He curled up on the bed and lay there purring. He was still purring softly to himself, when Tim at last went back to sleep.

On the way to school next morning, Tim told the others what had happened.

"But what are we going to do?" asked Simon. "Jared was going to get into the house for us."

"I'll have to do that," said Tim. "I've been thinking it all out. Two of us can go to Bargeman's Square, and get the silver things, and leave them for the policeman. And the other two will have to go to Piper's Farm.

"This is how we can work it. We'll do it tonight. I don't want to wait any longer, do you?"

Everyone agreed about that.

"All right, then," said Tim. "You must all be ready by half past eleven. Just before midnight, I'll come over to Simon and Jessica's house. I'll fly over with Sebastian on a broomstick.

"I shall have Melinda's drink with me. One drop of that drink makes you invisible for an hour. We'll all drink some of that. The Hidden People will still be able to see us, of course, and we can see each other. But the Ordinary Folk won't be able to see us, and we know that the burglars are Ordinary Folk.

"As soon as I get to Jessica's room, Sebastian can go over to Arun's house and bring Arun.

"Then I'll go off with Simon, and get the silver. Sebastian will take us. That's the best way, because then we can get into the house in Bargeman's Square through the skylight."

He turned to Arun and Jessica.

"As soon as we're inside," he said, "Sebastian can come back for you and bring you to the square.

"Simon and I can get some of the silver things. We'll let ourselves out of the door downstairs — or out of one of the downstairs windows.

"We'll meet you in the square. We'll give you some things to take to Piper's Farm. You can go off with Sebastian, and we'll wait in the square till the policeman comes. Then we'll put the silver on the pavement outside the house, so that he finds it. We can see what happens, and then go back to my house.

"When you've left the things in Piper's Farm, come back with Sebastian. I don't think the police will go to Piper's Farm before daylight. They'll have to question Kevin's uncle. There's no point in your waiting there. We'll all meet back in The Yard, in my room. O.K.?"

"O.K.!" said Simon.

"Does that sound all right, Arun?" asked Tim.

"I think so," said Arun thoughtfully. "Yes, that should be fine, Tim."

"Jessica?"

"I can't think of anything else, Tim," said Jessica.

"Good," said Tim. "See you later, then."

They turned in at the school gate.

* * *

None of them did very well in school that day. Arun and Tim both got into trouble for 'dreaming' — for not paying attention. Simon was so excited, that he kept knocking things over, and was finally sent out to run all around the school three times to cool off. And Jessica made so many mistakes in a story that she was writing, that she had to start it all over again from the beginning.

They were all thankful when at last school was over, and they could go home.

The evening dragged slowly by. In their separate houses, Tim and Arun, Jessica and Simon all tried to eat their suppers as if it was an ordinary night.

Auntie Lizzie was rather cross with Simon, because he couldn't sit still. Arun's mother thought he was looking tired, and told him to go to bed early. No one else noticed anything.

After supper, Tim went upstairs with Sebastian. He lay down on the bed in his clothes, and tried to get some sleep. But it was no good. He kept thinking and thinking of all the things they had to do.

At last it was time to start.

Tim had made sure that the broomstick was under his bed, before he had supper. Now he put on his anorak, opened his top drawer, and took out the little bottle Melinda had given him. He was already wearing the silver coin on a silver chain round his neck. (He had been wearing it all week, to make sure that he could see Jared and Tobias.) His hand touched the silver whistle — Melinda's gift. Tim pulled it out and put it in his pocket. He picked up the shoes from Piper's Farm which Jared had given him.

"All right, Sebastian," he said softly.

"Rrrr!" answered Sebastian.

He twitched his tail. The window fell open. The broomstick moved out into the room. Sebastian jumped on to it, and rode it through the open window.

Tim tied the laces of the shoes together. He hung the shoes round his neck. He climbed out of the window, and settled himself down on the broomstick.

"All right, Sebastian," he said. "We'll go and pick up Simon. This is it. Off you go."

Sebastian twitched his tail, and the broomstick moved out across The Yard.

Chapter Eight

Simon and Jessica were waiting by their window, which was already open. Sebastian held the broomstick steady while Tim climbed in. Then he went off to find Arun.

Tim had scarcely taken Melinda's bottle out of his pocket, before Sebastian and Arun arrived. This time, as soon as Arun had climbed in through the window, Sebastian flew the broomstick right into the room. He dropped it on the floor.

Tim unscrewed the top of the bottle, and poured five drops of the red liquid into the cap.

"Five drops will make anyone invisible for five hours," he said. "That should be long enough. We mustn't take too much, because we've got to be visible again by breakfast time."

Simon laughed. He was hopping up and down with excitement.

"Wouldn't it be fun if we weren't?" he said. "Just think what we could do! We could grab Auntie Lizzie's toast out of her hand, just as she was going to eat it. We could —"

"Shut up, Simon," said Tim. "We're not fooling around this time. You've got to think what you're doing. Whatever happens, don't fool around tonight. It's serious."

"All right," said Simon. "I'll be careful, Tim."

"Just think about what you're doing all the time," said Tim. "Here you are, Jessica. You drink this."

Jessica took the cap of the bottle, and drank the five drops.

"I can still see her," said Simon.

"Of course you can," said Tim. "This only makes you invisible to Ordinary Folk. You've got a magic coin, so you can see her. It's not like the drink Melinda gave her, when she had to go into Hollow Hill. *No one* could see her, after she'd drunk that — not even the Hidden People."

Jessica shivered. She remembered the time when she had had to go among the wild witches only too well.

"Tim," she said. "I've been thinking. Keep your gloves on, when you're in that house in Bargeman's Square. You too, Simon. The police will check the house for fingerprints. You don't want them to find yours."

"She's right," said Arun. "Did you have your gloves on, last time you were there, Tim?"

"Yes, I did," said Tim. "It was so cold. But that was a bit of luck. I hadn't thought about fingerprints."

He poured five more drops into the cap of the bottle.

"Here you are, Arun," he said.

Arun drank his five drops.

Tim gave five drops to Simon, and then drank five himself. The bottle was still half full. He put the cap on carefully, and put the bottle back in his pocket.

"How do I know if I'm invisible?" asked Simon.

"You're wearing your magic coin," said Tim. "I can see it through your sweater."

Simon looked down.

"I can see it too," he said.

"When you can see the magic coin shining through your sweater, you're invisible," said Tim. "When you can't, you're not. Everyone can see you again.

"Come on, Simon. We've got to go now. Arun and Jessica wait here. We'll send the broomstick back for you as soon as we're in the house in Bargeman's Square. Wait for us outside. We can get out of a downstairs door — or a downstairs window. We shan't be long."

Sebastian flicked his tail. The broomstick lifted off the floor. Sebastian rode it out of the window, and kept it hanging in the air outside while Tim and Simon climbed on.

"Good luck," whispered Arun.

"Thanks," said Tim softly. "See you later."

Sebastian waved his tail, and the broomstick flew off, over the roofs of the houses.

A few minutes later, they were at the skylight in the roof of the house in Bargeman's Square. The street lamp was on, and they could see quite well.

Sebastian twitched his tail hard. Tim heard the catch on the skylight click open. He lifted it up.

"Climb in while I hold it open," he whispered softly to Simon. "There's a ladder against the wall inside. Climb down it, and wait for me. Don't make a sound! They should be asleep by this time, but you never know."

Simon climbed in.

Tim gave him a few moments, and then climbed on to the top of the ladder himself.

"All right, Sebastian," he whispered. "You can fetch the others now. Give us ten minutes, and then meet us in the square."

Sebastian flew off into the night.

Tim shut the skylight down softly. He climbed carefully down the ladder.

He pulled out his torch, and flashed it on. Simon was waiting.

"Sh!" breathed Tim. "Don't make a sound."

He switched off his torch, turned the handle of the door, and stepped out into the landing. The house was dark and silent.

"Come on," he whispered to Simon. "Put your hand on the banisters and feel your way along to the stairs."

He crept softly along the landing. As he came to the head of the stairs, he could hear deep breathing coming from the front room. It wasn't exactly snoring, but someone was very deeply asleep.

They crept down the stairs. Half-way down, one of the stairs creaked loudly.

Tim stopped. He stood quite still. His heart was beating wildly. The sounds from the front bedroom stopped. There was a kind of snort. Tim and Simon stood as if they had been turned to stone.

There were heaving sounds, as if someone was turning over in bed.

They waited.

After a minute or two, the deep breathing began again. It really was snoring, this time.

Tim crept on. He came to the bottom of the stairs.

"Turn to the right," he breathed to Simon. "This way."

They crept along the passage. Tim opened the door at the top of the cellar stairs. Simon went through. Tim followed him and shut the door silently behind them. He switched on his torch.

"We can use this, now," he whispered. "Be careful. We still mustn't make a sound."

They went down the steps. Tim turned the handle of the door into the room where the silver things were. The door wouldn't open. It was locked.

"What do we do now?" whispered Simon.

"I think I know where the key is," whispered Tim. "Wait here for me. I'll get it."

He made his way back up the steps, and into the hall. The sound of snoring was louder than ever.

Tim switched on his torch, and saw the little table in the hall. There was a telephone standing on it, with a white memo pad and a pencil beside it.

Tim was just going to open the drawer in the table, to get the key, when he had an idea.

He picked up the pencil, and printed on the memo pad: KEVIN AND JIM. PIPER'S FARM. He was a bit clumsy, because he kept his gloves on, but the printing was quite clear.

He put down the pencil, and opened the table drawer. There was the key. He pulled it out, switched off his torch, and shut the drawer softly.

With the key still in his hand, he tiptoed back to the cellar.

"I think this is it," he said to Simon.

He fitted the key into the lock. It turned. Tim opened the door and they went into the room.

He flashed his torch round. It looked just as it had looked when he had seen it the first time. The boxes of silver lay on the table. The shelves were full of silver candlesticks, vases and bowls. There were radios stacked at one side.

Tim took the shoes from Piper's Farm, which were still hanging around his neck, and put them under the table.

"What a place!" whispered Simon.

"I don't think they can have done a job since I was here before," said Tim. "It looks just the same.

"Now, let's take that vase. That's the kind of thing anyone would recognise."

He pointed to a silver vase. It was tall, and it had a silver snake twisted round it.

"Look at that ship!" exclaimed Simon.

"Sh!" whispered Tim. "You must whisper, Simon. Anyone might hear us. Yes. That ship's just the thing. It's the sort of thing Kevin and Jim might take with them."

It was a little silver ship with silver sails. Tiny silver sailors were on deck. It was a beautiful thing.

"Put a few of those spoons in your pocket, too," whispered Tim. "The ones with the dragons on them. That's plenty. Come on."

They went out into the cellar, and Tim shut the door softly behind him and locked it.

"I'm going to leave the key in the lock," he whispered. "Come on."

They crept back up the cellar steps to the hall.

"The back door's this way," breathed Tim.

The back door was to their right. Tim made sure that the cellar door was shut. Then he shone his torch on the back door. It had a lock and two bolts.

The key was in the lock. He reached up, and softly slid back the top bolt. Then he slid the bottom bolt. He couldn't help making a bit of noise with them. They were old bolts, and the metal clicked as he moved them.

He stood still and listened. Faint sounds of snoring drifted down the stairs.

Tim turned the key. There was a loud click as the lock went back. He stopped.

"Keep still," he whispered to Simon. Simon was dancing from one foot to the other beside him in excitement.

Simon kept his feet still and bit his lower lip instead.

The house was still silent, except for the snoring above.

Tim turned the handle, and they let themselves out into the road that came into Bargeman's Square.

Tim shut the door softly behind them. He switched off his torch. The street lamp was still on, and there was no need for it. They went down to the corner. Arun and Jessica were waiting for them, with Sebastian and the broomstick.

"Everything all right, Tim?" whispered Arun.

Tim nodded.

"Here you are," he whispered. "Give them the ship, Simon. And here's a vase. We've got some spoons. We're going to scatter the spoons on the pavement, as if they'd been dropped by mistake."

Arun took the little silver ship, and Jessica took the vase. Sebastian flicked his tail, and the broomstick lifted off the ground.

"We'll walk back to The Yard," said Tim. "Don't send Sebastian for us, unless you need us. He can always fetch us, if anything happens.

"But if everything's all right, we'll see you back at The Yard later. We shan't leave until we see what the police do."

"All right," said Arun. "See you later, then, Tim."

Sebastian waved his tail, and the broomstick flew off.

Chapter Nine

"It must be nearly time for the policeman to make his rounds," whispered Tim. "We'll scatter the spoons here, just in front of the house. But we'll wait till we see the policeman come into The Yard. And then do it softly. Put each spoon down carefully on the pavement. We don't want the policeman to hear us."

"O.K.," breathed Simon.

Tim took a look at the front of the house.

"Just about here, I think," he whispered.

He looked at the window of the basement room. It was heavily barred, and the red curtain was drawn across inside, as usual.

Tim drew in his breath.

"I'm stupid!" he whispered. "You know what we ought to have done, Simon? We ought to have pulled that curtain back. The policeman will flash his torch around when he finds the spoons. If we'd pulled that curtain back just a little bit, he'd have seen the rest of the silver inside."

"Let's go back and do it," said Simon.

"The policeman may come any moment now," said Tim. "One of us has to stay here. I'll go back in. The back door's still open.

"You stay here. If the policeman comes before I get back, put the spoons down here on the pavement. And *put* them down, Simon. Don't drop them. Don't make a sound. And then move off a bit and watch. I won't be long."

"All right," said Simon.

Tim went round to the back door. Simon stood on the pavement with the spoons in his hand, watching and waiting.

Tim opened the back door softly, and let himself into the hall. He closed the door behind him. He stood still for a moment, listening. He could still hear the faint sound of snoring from upstairs.

He found the door to the cellar, and crept down the steps. He unlocked the door into the front room, and went in. He flashed on his torch for a moment, to see his way round the table, and then put it off again. He didn't want anyone to see a light in the basement room just then.

His hand groped along the wall. He felt the curtain, and jerked it back a little. A streak of light from the street lamp outside shone into the room. He pulled the curtain just a little further back, so that it looked as if someone had been careless in pulling it across the window. He could see Simon through the crack, standing on the pavement outside.

Tim made his way back round the table into the cellar, shutting the door behind him.

He had got to the top of the cellar steps, when he tripped and fell. He never knew for certain what it was that he fell over, but it felt like a broom.

There was a great crash. Tim and a bucket both tumbled down the steps together.

Tim picked himself up. His ankle hurt a bit,

but he didn't seem to have broken anything. His one idea now was to get out.

He raced up the steps again and out into the back hall. He heard a door open above. Suddenly, the lights came on in the hall and on the landing.

"Who's there?" a deep voice cried. "Who's there? You'd better keep still, whoever you are. I've got a gun, and I'll use it."

Tim swiftly shut the cellar door, and stepped into the kitchen, which was just opposite.

Heavy steps were coming downstairs. The big man he had seen before came along the passage and looked into the kitchen. The gun was in his hand.

The big man went to the cellar door, opened it, and clicked on a switch. He looked down into the cellar.

He stepped back, and looked at the back door. He stepped quickly over to it, shot the bolts back into position, and turned the key in the lock. He put the key in his pocket, and went back to the cellar steps. His gun was at the ready.

He went down into the cellar. Tim heard his grunt of surprise, as he found the key down there.

Tim heard the door to the basement room open. He waited for the sound of the curtain being pulled again, but it didn't come. The big man was so busy checking the silver, that he hadn't noticed the window.

Tim heard him shut the door and lock it. He was coming upstairs again. Tim slipped quickly out of the kitchen and into the front hall.

The man came up the steps. Then he got a chair, and put it down in a corner of the hall, near the stairs, where he could see both the front and the back doors.

He sat down, with his gun at the ready, listening.

Tim bit his lip. He must get out somehow. Simon would have seen the lights go on in the house, and he would be worried. If Tim didn't appear soon, Simon might try and rescue him. And then what would happen? Simon might miss the policeman, and things could so easily go wrong. He might even get shot.

The big man put down his gun for a moment, and lit a cigarette.

Tim looked at the front door. He couldn't go out that way, and he couldn't go out through the back door. The man would hear him. He would see the doors open, and he might shoot, even if he couldn't see who he was shooting at. The only safe way out was through the skylight.

Tim moved very softly forwards. He passed

within a metre of the man, and began to go upstairs. He remembered the stair which creaked, and stepped over it.

Tim must have made some little sounds, because the man looked at the stairs several times. He turned his head as if he were listening. But he stayed sitting where he was.

Tim got to the top of the stairs. He crossed the landing and opened the boxroom door. He crept into the boxroom, and shut the door behind him. He listened. There was no sound from below.

Tim felt his way to the ladder, climbed up, and opened the skylight. He climbed through, and shut the skylight softly down behind him. He gave a great sigh of relief. At least he was out of the house. The only difficulty was, that he was up on the roof, when he wanted to be on the ground. If only Sebastian had been there!

He remembered the silver whistle. He had it in his pocket. Melinda had given it to him, and it was magic. He had only to blow that whistle, and Sebastian would hear it, wherever he was.

Tim thought for a moment. Arun and Jessica were probably at Piper's Farm by this time. Even if they weren't, Sebastian could put them down, and pick them up again later. He must get down from the roof, before Simon did anything dangerous. It would be just like Simon to try to get into the house to rescue him.

Tim pulled out the whistle, and blew it.

He heard nothing at all, but Melinda had said that he wouldn't be able to hear it. He blew it again, and then slipped it back into his pocket, and waited.

Tim looked down into the square. It was empty. He couldn't see Simon, and he daren't call out to him, in case the big man heard him. He heard a clock somewhere in the town strike half past twelve.

* * *

A quarter of an hour later, Tim saw a broomstick sail over the roof of a house opposite, and in another moment, Sebastian was beside him.

"Rrrrr?" asked Sebastian.

"Sebastian! I'm so glad to see you," exclaimed Tim. "The man in the house is up, and he's got a gun, and I had to climb out this way. Simon's in the square. Take me down to him, and then you can go back to Jessica and Arun. Are they all right?"

"Rrrr!" said Sebastian.

Tim climbed on to the broomstick, Sebastian twitched his tail, and half a minute later Tim was standing in the street beside Simon.

"What happened?" asked Simon. "I was just going to come in to find you."

"That's what I was afraid of," said Tim. "The big man's up, and he's got a gun."

Simon lifted his hand. "Listen!" he said.

They heard the sound of footsteps, coming down one of the roads into the square.

"Off you go, Sebastian," whispered Tim. "Go back to Arun and Jessica. We'll be all right now."

Sebastian jumped on to the broomstick, and flew up over the nearest roof.

A policeman came out of one of the streets into the square.

"Put the spoons down," breathed Tim.

He took some from Simon, and together they set them down silently on the pavement.

It was hard to remember that the policeman couldn't see them. He was walking straight towards them.

Tim put down the last spoon. He straightened up, and joined Simon, who was already standing out in the square, watching.

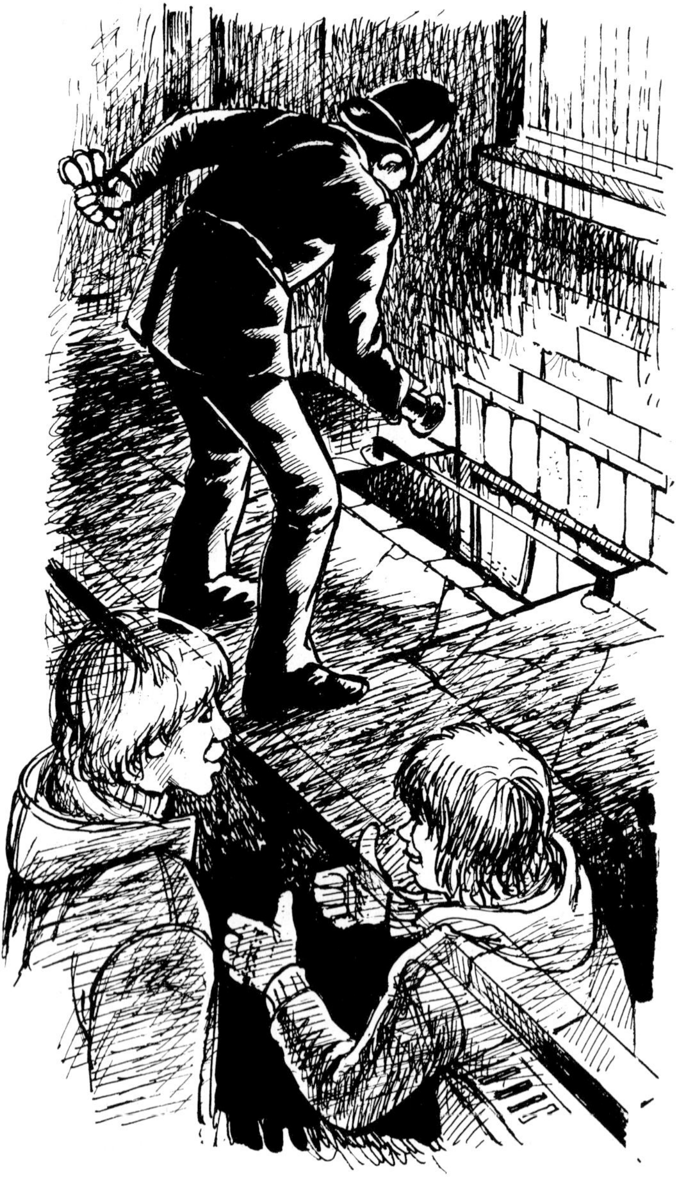

The policeman came nearer and nearer.

They could see the spoons shining in the light of the street lamp. He must see them.

The policeman stopped. He took out a torch, and shone it on to the pavement. The spoons glittered. He stooped down and picked them up.

Then he flashed his torch around, just as Tim had hoped he would, to see if there were any more.

Suddenly, he stiffened. He had seen the window. He bent down to look through the crack in the curtain, shining his torch into the room.

Simon touched Tim's arm. Tim glanced at him. Simon held up both his thumbs in triumph.

Tim nodded and grinned.

The policeman was talking into his walkie-talkie. He was speaking quietly, and they couldn't hear everything, but they caught the words "silver" and "search warrant".

The policeman put the walkie-talkie away, and moved into the shadow at the end of the houses. He stood so that he could see both the back and the front door of the house where the silver was.

They waited. The time seemed to crawl by. They heard a clock strike one, and then quarter past.

Two police cars came into the square. The policemen got out, and went over to the house. They joined the first policeman on the pavement.

The lights in the house were still on. The policemen took a quick look through the crack in the curtain. Then one of them went to the front door. He knocked.

The door was flung open by the big man.

"What do you want at this time of night?" he growled.

"Good evening, sir," said the policeman. "I found these on the pavement. Are they yours?"

The big man stared at the spoons.

"No," he said. "No. I've never seen them before."

"Perhaps we could come in for a minute," said the policeman. "No need to wake the neighbours."

For a moment Tim thought the big man was going to slam the door in the policeman's face. Tim wondered where the gun was. Then the big man saw the police cars. He stepped back. Another policeman moved forward to join the one at the door, and they both went inside.

"That's done it," whispered Simon. "They'll find everything now."

Tim nodded.

The policemen in the other car had been talking over their radio.

After a few minutes, they drove off.

Tim and Simon waited quietly in the shadows.

The door of the house opened, and two policemen came out. The big man was with them. He was dressed. He looked angry, and at the same time he looked afraid.

He got into the back of the police car, and a policeman got in with him. The other one got into the driver's seat, and they drove off.

There was still one policeman at the house — the one who had found the spoons. He shut the door of the house, and stood outside it.

Tim shivered. It was very cold.

"Come on, Simon," he whispered. "We may as well go home now. The others will be back from the farm."

"Can't we wait and see what happens next?" asked Simon.

"I expect they'll wait till morning now," said Tim. "Then they'll send their experts along, to look for fingerprints and take pictures. But we shan't be able to see that, anyway, because it will all be inside. And I want to hear what's happened to the others."

"All right," said Simon. "I bet they're back by now."

They walked through the dark streets, across the bridge over the canal, and back to The Yard.

There was always a key under the stone by the front steps of Tim's house. Tim got it, and opened the front door very softly. He didn't want to wake Aunt May.

They went inside. Tim put the key back again. He shut the front door and crept quietly upstairs to his room, with Simon close behind him.

Tim thought that the others might have got there already, but the attic was empty.

Tim shut the door, and switched on the light. They sat down to wait.

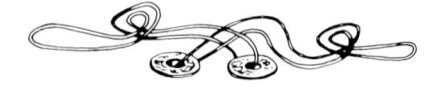

Chapter Ten

It was cold, but the night was clear.

Jessica looked down over the dark roofs of the town, as Sebastian flew the broomstick swiftly along. Arun was sitting behind her. Sebastian stood on the front of the broomstick, as if he were standing on the prow of a ship.

They could see the street lights below them. The traffic lights at the crossroads shone red and green. Here and there, a window glowed in the darkness.

Sebastian followed the line of the canal. Soon, they left the buildings and factories behind them. Jessica could see the fields and trees below them in the moonlight.

"There's Hollow Hill," said Arun softly. "We're not far from Piper's Wood now."

"Do you know where the farm is?" asked Jessica, looking back at him.

Arun shook his head.

"No," he said. "But Sebastian does. He'll take us there. But I should watch to see which way we go. We'll want to be able to find it ourselves, later."

Jessica looked down, and saw the little bridge over the canal ahead of them.

"There's Piper's Wood," she said. "And look! There's Melinda's house. There's a light in her window."

They saw the little house below them. Jessica felt much better, knowing that Melinda was there. They were flying out into the dark, and they didn't know quite where they were going, but they had a friend not far away. Melinda was there.

They flew over Piper's Wood, and then above the road. Arun saw a pool of water in a field below them to their left. He guessed that it must be the pool with the whispering trees. Tim had told him about that pool.

Sebastian swung the broomstick over to the right.

"Look!" said Jessica, pointing. "That must be it."

An old stone farmhouse stood in the middle of one of the fields, about half a mile off the road. There was a white gate on the road, and a farm lane leading to it. There was a big farmyard, with stone barns on two sides of it.

The broomstick was coming down.

Suddenly, the broomstick shot up about ten feet, with a great jerk, which nearly tipped them off.

It swung round.

"Rrrrrr," cried Sebastian.

The broomstick pointed downwards, towards a clump of trees and bushes.

"What is it?" cried Jessica.

"We're going down," said Arun. "Hold on. Sebastian's seen something."

They came down among the trees. Sebastian held the broomstick a little way above the ground, while they got off.

They expected him to jump off too. But the moment they were safely on the ground,

Sebastian and the broomstick shot off into the air, back the way they had come.

Jessica and Arun stood staring after him.

"I know what's happened!" said Jessica. "It's Tim! He's called Sebastian back. He's blown the silver whistle that Melinda gave him."

"I expect you're right," said Arun. "I hope Tim's not in any trouble."

"What shall we do?" said Jessica.

"I think we'd better wait for a bit," said Arun. "Sebastian will know how to get into the farmhouse. We don't.

"Let's wait for a bit, and see if he comes back. If he doesn't, we can try and get into the house ourselves. And if we can't do that, we can hide the silver in one of the barns. I expect the police will search the whole place, once they get here."

There was an old tree trunk lying on the grass by some bushes. They sat down on it, and waited.

The time passed slowly. It was very cold. Jessica rubbed her hands together, trying to keep them warm. She was feeling very scared. She had been a bit frightened at the thought of going into the strange farmhouse. But now, having nothing to do, she felt worse than ever.

Arun seemed to guess what she was feeling. He began to talk to her about the stars. He knew the names of many of them, and he pointed them out to her.

They had got up and moved out from under the trees, to look at the pole star, when Arun suddenly gripped Jessica's arm. He pulled her back, close to some high bushes.

"Look, Jessica!" he whispered suddenly. "Look! *What's that?*"

Three dark shapes sailed across the sky over them. Each figure was wearing a tall, pointed hat. Three long cloaks blew out in the wind.

"Witches!" breathed Jessica. "Witches!"

"Have you got your box with you?" Arun whispered softly.

Jessica shook her head.

"I've left it at home," she said. "I never thought we'd need it — not now."

Melinda had given Jessica a magic gift — a box, which played a tune when she lifted the lid. When the tune was played, a wind blew. If there were any witches about, they were blown away on the wind. But the box was standing on the table by Jessica's bed, in the house in The Yard.

"Did the witches come from Piper's Farm?" she whispered.

"No," said Arun. "I don't expect they're anything to do with the burglars. But they must be up to something. Perhaps that's why Melinda wanted Jared and Tobias."

He thought for a moment.

"I don't think we've anything to worry about, Jessica," he said. "They're not after us."

There was a cheerful little purr, and Sebastian rode the broomstick down beside them.

"Rrrr?" he said, as he held it hovering in the air.

"Oh, Sebastian, I'm so glad you're back!" cried Jessica.

"We'll have to be careful, Sebastian," said Arun. "There are witches about. Keep your eyes open."

"Rrrr!" said Sebastian.

They got on to the broomstick. Sebastian twitched his tail. They sailed up into the air again, and over towards the farmhouse.

Sebastian circled the house, and then brought the broomstick in close to one of the windows.

Arun looked at the window. It was just ajar.

He peered in, and saw that the window was on a landing.

"It's a good place," he whispered. "I'll climb in first. Then you come, Jess. Sebastian, wait here for us with the broomstick."

Arun leaned over, lifted the catch, and gently pulled the window wide open. He climbed through, and Jessica followed him.

Arun switched on a torch. They were standing on a landing, with doors on each side of it. Stairs led down to the hall.

Arun shone his torch down the stairs. He touched Jessica's arm, and pointed. There was an old chest standing in the hall.

They crept downstairs. Arun lifted the lid of the chest. There was just a rug inside it. He pulled the silver boat out from under his sweater, lifted the edge of the rug, and pushed the boat under it. Jessica handed him the vase, and he pushed that under the rug, too.

He switched off his torch, and shut the chest very gently. They crept back up the stairs.

"You wait here by the window," he breathed softly to Jessica. "I'm going to make sure that it's the right house."

Jessica waited.

Arun opened the first door, and looked into the room. He shut it again, and went to the next door. This time he went right into the room.

A moment later, he came out, closing the door softly behind him.

"It's Piper's Farm all right," he breathed into Jessica's ear, as he came back to the window. "Kevin and Jim are sleeping in that room. Come on. We'll get back to Tim."

They climbed out of the window, on to the waiting broomstick. Arun leant back, and put the window back on its catch.

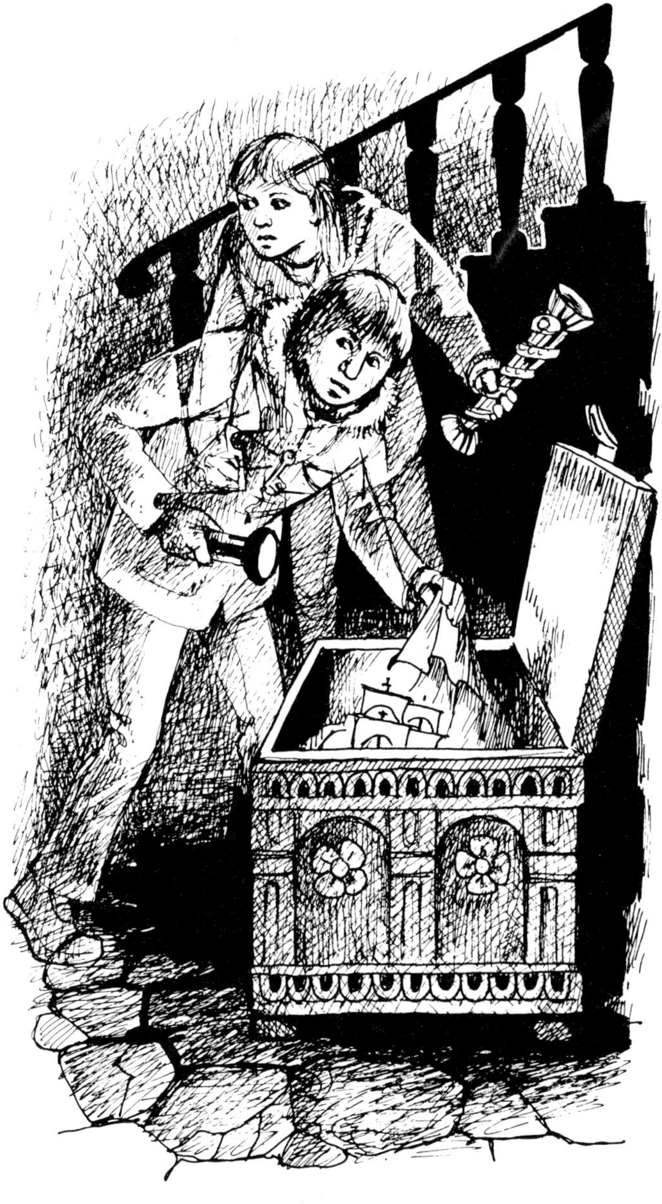

"All set, Sebastian," he said softly, as he gripped the broomstick again. "Jim and Kevin are there, and we've left the silver. Let's go home."

Sebastian gave a soft purr. He twitched his tail, and the broomstick sailed off into the night.

*   *   *

They saw no witches, on their way back to The Yard. Everything below them was dark and still, until they came to the lights of the town.

Sebastian took the broomstick over the roofs to Tim's window. Tim and Simon were waiting, to help them to climb in.

"How did you get on?" Simon and Jessica said to each other at the same moment.

They all laughed.

"Fine," said Arun. "Sebastian found the farm. Jim and Kevin were there, sleeping. We've left the silver in an old chest.

"How about you? You called Sebastian back, didn't you? What happened?"

Tim told him about the man with the gun, and how the police had come.

"I wonder if they'll find out about Piper's Farm," said Simon. "That man won't tell them."

"I printed Jim and Kevin's names on the memo pad by the telephone," said Tim. "And I printed 'Piper's Farm' on the pad, too. It's there as if it was something he had to remember. I printed it in capitals, so that they wouldn't know my writing."

"That was brilliant, Tim," said Arun. "Really brilliant!"

Tim grinned.

"It was just a sudden idea," he said.

"How long will we be invisible?" asked Simon.

"Not long now," said Arun. "It's not long now till morning. We'd better be getting home."

"I've got something for us to eat, first," said Tim. "Just to celebrate."

He opened his drawer, and took out some apples and a slab of chocolate.

"I thought we'd be hungry," he said.

They were hungry. The chocolate and apples disappeared quickly. Even Sebastian ate a square of chocolate.

When they had finished, they finally got up to go. Nobody really wanted to go home, but everyone was beginning to feel very tired.

"We'd better get some sleep," said Arun. "Tim and I might cycle over to Piper's Farm in the morning, and see if anything's happening."

"It's morning now," said Simon.

"So it is," said Arun. "Come on, Jessica. You and Simon first. Sebastian will take you home."

Sebastian took Simon and Jessica across The Yard to their own house, and then came back for Arun.

By the time Tim had got into his pyjamas, and climbed into bed, Sebastian was back from

Arun's house. He sailed in through the window, dropped the broomstick on the floor, and jumped up on to Tim's bed purring loudly.

Tim got up and hid the broomstick under the bed.

"You've been terrific, Sebastian," said Tim. "We'd never have done it without you."

Tim climbed back into bed and Sebastian snuggled down beside him, still purring. Tim curled up and went to sleep.

Chapter Eleven

Tim didn't wake until Aunt May opened the door of his bedroom, and looked in to see where he was.

"Tim!" she said. "Tim! Wake up!"

He opened his eyes.

"Do you know what the time is?" asked Aunt May. "It's nearly one o'clock! You've slept all morning. I've been up three times to look at you."

"You should have woken me," said Tim.

"You must have needed your sleep," said Aunt May. "You've been looking tired lately. There was nothing for you to get up for.

"But it's dinner time now. You've missed your breakfast. You'd better come and have your dinner."

"I was going out with Arun," said Tim, thinking of Piper's Farm.

"Well, you can go out with him this afternoon," said Aunt May. "Arun came to call for you, but I wouldn't let him wake you."

She went downstairs.

Tim got dressed.

He ate his dinner as quickly as he could, and then ran across The Yard to see Arun.

Arun opened the door.

"Hallo, Tim," he said.

"Did you go to the farm?" asked Tim.

"No," said Arun. "I started out. I was half-way there when two police cars passed me. So I turned back. They passed me on the way back, too, just as I was nearly in the town. Kevin and Jim were in one of them.''

"So we've done it!" said Tim.

"Yes, we've done it," said Arun. "I've told Jessica and Simon. I think they're sleeping it all off, this afternoon."

"I slept in this morning," said Tim.

"I'm dropping asleep now," said Arun.

Tim went back to his house, and left Arun to sleep. He was still feeling tired himself.

* * *

Tim and Aunt May had just finished breakfast on Sunday morning, when a police car came into The Yard. It stopped outside Mr. Berryman's house.

One of the policemen got out, and knocked on the front door. Mr. Berryman opened it, and the policeman went inside.

The other policeman got out, and came across The Yard. He came through the gate. They heard him ring the front door bell.

"What does he want this time?" said Aunt May. "And on Sunday morning, too!"

She bustled up the stairs, taking her apron off as she went. Tim went up behind her.

"Well?" asked Aunt May, as she opened the door. "What is it?"

"Good morning, Miss McNair," said the policeman. "I just thought that I'd look in to tell you that we've caught the burglars. And Tim's in the clear.

"I'm sorry we had to come and ask the boy a lot of questions. But we do have to ask questions, when there's a burglary. We have to find out who did it, for everyone's sake, especially when someone's been hurt.

"But I thought you'd like to know that it's all cleared up now."

He saw Tim standing behind her.

"Hallo, Tim," he said. "You've nothing to worry about now. One of them's confessed. He's told us everything. We know who did it, and we know what happened."

Tim grinned. The policeman might think he knew what had happened, but he certainly didn't know everything.

"*Of course* Tim hasn't anything to worry about," said Aunt May. "He never had. He never did anything wrong."

She looked fiercely at the policeman.

The policeman smiled at her.

"Well, it's nice of you to come and tell me, anyway," said Aunt May.

"That's all right," said the policeman. "We were just seeing Mr. Berryman, and I thought you'd like to know. But don't go looking for burglars again, will you, Tim?"

Tim just grinned. He said nothing.

"How's that poor old lady who lived in Baker's Lane?" asked Aunt May. "Mrs. Kelsey, wasn't it? Didn't they have to take her to hospital?"

"She's much better," said the policeman. "She broke her arm, and she was very shaken up, but she's going to be all right."

"Well, that's a good thing," said Aunt May. "I think it's really wicked, to go hitting an old lady like that. They're lucky they didn't kill her."

"Very lucky," said the policeman.

He went back to the car.

"There, now," said Aunt May. "I knew you had nothing to do with it, Tim. But I suppose they did have to ask questions."

The other policeman came out of Mr. Berryman's house, and the car drove away.

Aunt May went back downstairs. Mr. Berryman came across The Yard, and Tim went down the steps to meet him.

"Well, Tim, they've caught the burglars," said Mr. Berryman. "I expect the policeman told you."

"Yes," said Tim.

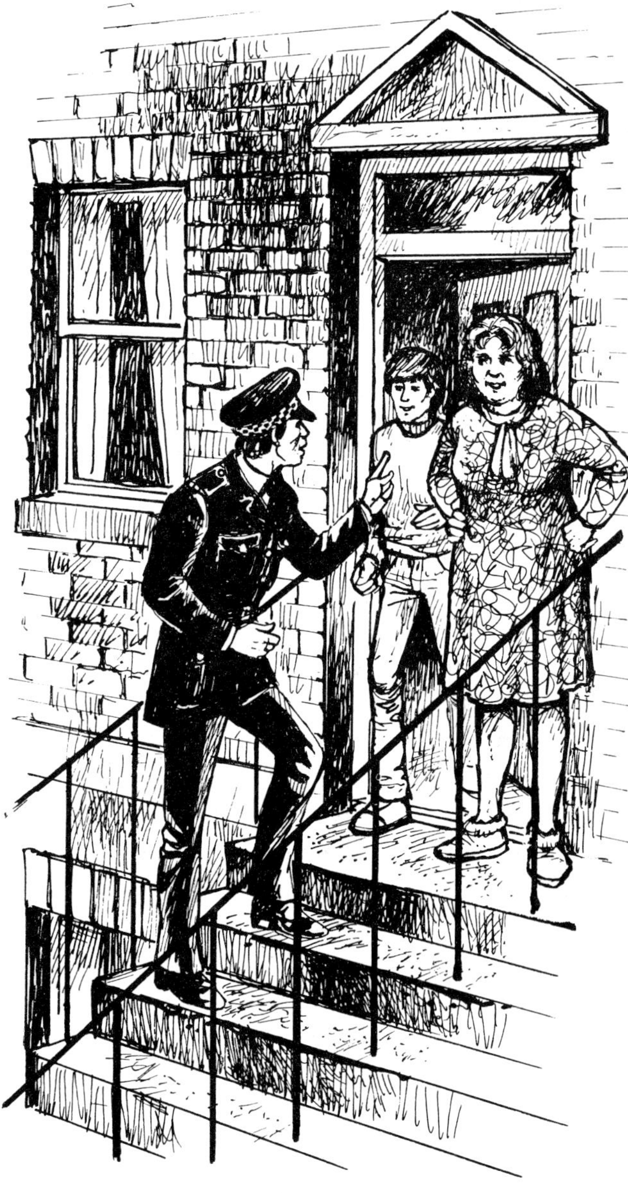

"I'm glad they've been caught," said Mr. Berryman. "And I'm glad for you, too, Tim. I never believed you could have had a hand in those burglaries. But I'm glad you're in the clear, boy. It's better that everyone should know who did it. Better for everyone's sake."

Tim said nothing.

"You know, Tim," said Mr. Berryman. "There's still one thing I can't understand. Why did the burglars bring back my spoons?"

Tim looked at him quickly. He said nothing at all.

"Tim," said Mr. Berryman. "I know you had nothing to do with the burglaries. I know you wouldn't hurt anyone. You're not that kind of boy. But it would be just like you, to see that I got my spoons back, if you had found where the burglars had hidden them. Did you, Tim? Did you try to help me?"

Tim looked at Mr. Berryman. Mr. Berryman was looking at him in a very kindly way. He remembered how kind Mr. Berryman had always been. He decided to trust him.

"It *was* something like that, Mr. Berryman," he said. "But please don't tell anyone."

"Ah!" said Mr. Berryman. "I thought so. I won't tell anyone, Tim, if you don't want me to. You can trust me. And I won't ask any more questions. But you must have taken a big risk, to try to help me. I shan't forget.

"Well, I hope we shall have a bit of peace and quiet now. It'll soon be Easter. It should be a bit warmer by then. You'll be able to have a holiday — a nice, quiet holiday. That's what you need."

Mr. Berryman went back to his house.

Tim looked thoughtful.

"A nice, quiet holiday," he said to himself. He remembered what Arun and Jessica had told him, about the three witches who had flown overhead. He wondered again, why Melinda had sent for Tobias and Jared.

"A nice, quiet holiday," he repeated. "I don't believe it. It couldn't happen! I wouldn't even be surprised if Tobias came looking for us tonight, to take us to Melinda!"

Tim went inside, and shut the door.

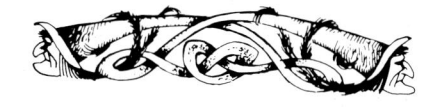